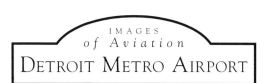

IMAGES
of Aviation

DETROIT METRO AIRPORT

TO MIKE
I hope you enjoy this book
as much as I did
the research 2/4/12

Daniel W. Mason

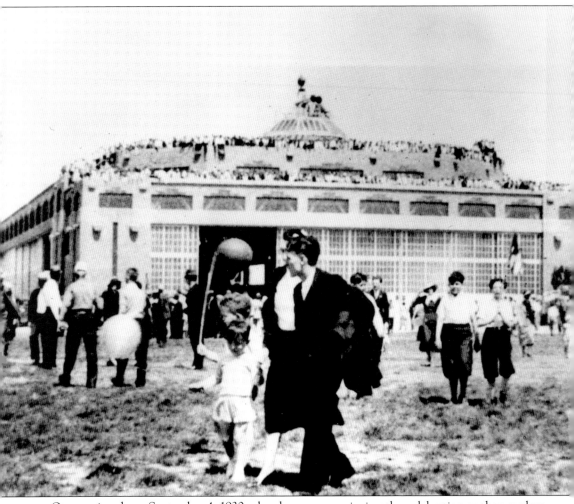

On opening day—September 4, 1930—locals are seen enjoying the celebration as they explore Wayne County Airport. This was the "golden age of flight," and people were curious as to what flying was all about and how it would take shape in southeastern Michigan. (Wayne County Airport Authority.)

ON THE COVER: Passengers wait to board their flight outside the new terminal at Detroit-Wayne Major Airport in 1952. (WCAA)

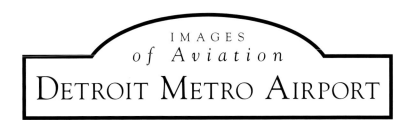

IMAGES
of Aviation

DETROIT METRO AIRPORT

Daniel W. Mason

ARCADIA
PUBLISHING

Published by Arcadia Publishing
Charleston, South Carolina

Printed in the United States of America

Library of Congress Control Number: 2011939317

For all general information, please contact Arcadia Publishing:
Telephone 843-853-2070
Fax 843-853-0044
E-mail sales@arcadiapublishing.com
For customer service and orders:
Toll-Free 1-888-313-2665

Visit us on the Internet at www.arcadiapublishing.com

This book is dedicated to the men and women who served at the Romulus Army Airfield during World War II and the Air National Guardsmen who served in Romulus while protecting our country—thank you.

CONTENTS

ACKNOWLEDGMENTS

I would like to thank the many people who helped me obtain information for this book. Thanks to Sarah Rickman, another author doing research about the Women Airforce Service Pilots (WASP) who served out of Romulus during World War II. She was a real help, and every time we talked about this book I found myself looking in another place I had not thought of for further research. Another new friend, Richard L. Story, curator of the Wayne Historical Museum, said when we first met, "You're gonna like what I've got, and you'll keep coming back again and again!" And he was right. Thanks to Scott Wintner and Scott Roberts from the Wayne County Airport Authority division of public affairs—I really appreciate their time and patience in letting me go through old photographs and news clippings and letting me explore behind-the-scenes parts of the airport. And thanks to Kenneth M. Kucel, the director of the engineering department at the Wayne County Department of Public Services.

Thanks to Jim Koglin, from the Selfridge Military Air Museum, for technical information about the Air National Guard and whose stories of the guard I enjoyed; Paul Nowak, retired deputy with the Wayne County Sheriff's Department, and his photographs of the Mounted Sheriffs Division; and Beth Van Duyne, from LSG Sky Chef. Thanks to the following people at FedEx: Dave Seaton, senior manager of ramp operations, Detroit, Michigan; Eric Borer, senior security specialist, Detroit, Michigan; Matt Dirette, manager of ramp operations; Sally Davenport, senior communications specialist, FedEx media relations; Steve Cook, senior communications specialist and staff photographer at FedEx corporate communications; and many others that I work with at FedEx. I would also like to thank the St. Louis Public Library; I guess I sparked some renewed interest in Adela Scharr, one of its old patrons.

Keith Jarvie, thanks for the tour of the Transportation Security Administration (TSA) operation and introducing some of the K-9 trainers and their partners. Thanks to British Airways Heritage Centre at London Heathrow Airport for the de Havilland Comet photograph. Thanks to Bruce Kitt from the NWA History Centre for the Northwest plane photograph and for his connection to Terry Love and his Republic Airlines photograph. Last but not least, thanks to my little sister Marilyn for her help in scanning and photograph repair.

INTRODUCTION

Detroit Metropolitan Airport has served the Detroit area for over 80 years. Originally, one hangar and a Michigan Air National Guard building occupied one square mile of land; the two lighted runways were state of the art at the time. Edward Hines, the president of the board of the Wayne County Road Commission, foresaw that the airport was going to be a significant part of the community in terms of jobs and transportation. Leroy Smith was there for the conception and through expansion in the 1950s, and he became president of the board in 1948.

By the beginning of World War II, the US Army Air Corps realized it would need bases to ferry various aircraft across the United States, thus Wayne County Airport, in Romulus, Michigan, became the Romulus Army Airfield. The runways were ready, and three main structures were already in place. In 1940 and 1941, part of the airport was leased for the base, and the corps took full responsibility for maintenance of the entire airport. Additional structures were built on the grounds, and hangars, warehouses, administration buildings, and barracks were constructed on new land acquired by the military. During the war, the 3rd Ferry Group was stationed in Romulus, which included the Women's Air Ferry Service (WAFS); 108 women served, proving they could fly just as well as men. The WAFS was disbanded by the end of 1944.

After the war, the Army returned the airport to the county, and plans were drawn up for expansion. Three more miles of property were acquired around the airport, and three new runways and a more modern terminal were erected. The airport was renamed Detroit-Wayne Major Airport in 1947. Passenger aircraft were entering the jet age, and with government aid and tax dollars from local citizens Wayne County expanded the existing terminal. It functioned like a small city, offering a bank, barbershop, restaurants, car dealerships, and a variety of small shops. By 1957, the airport had its first commercial jet and was forever changed. As time passed, many airlines came and went, with some remaining into the 21st century. A year later, the airport made a final name change to what it is currently known as—Detroit Metropolitan Wayne County Airport, or Detroit Metro Airport.

The Michigan Air National Guard maintained a presence at the airport until 1971, and a Nike base was maintained there during the Cold War. The airport was a strategic point, as it was important to protect the industrial heart of the United States. After 1971, the base was used for commercial use at the airport but eventually torn down for a new runway—only the old headquarters on Middlebelt Road remains. The airport would continue to grow and expand with the eventual construction of the McNamara and Midfield Terminals.

The images in this book appear courtesy of the following people and/or institutions:

One

WAYNE COUNTY AIRPORT

In 1927, state legislation was passed (Act 182, PA 1927) that authorized political subdivisions to acquire land for the operation of an airport. The board of supervisors of Wayne County formed a five-member committee, which advertised in newspapers that it was looking for suitable land for a major commercial airport. Proposals were submitted for 70 sites, and the committee decided that it would use the property at the corner of Goddard and Middlebelt Roads. A $2 million bond—which was in excess of the amount legally needed—was voted on by the public and approved for the construction of the airport. Construction began in 1929 and was completed in 1930. Two buildings were erected: the main hangar and a new Air National Guard facility.

The airport was located in a rural area both to ensure a buffer in case of accidents and to allow for expansion. Extensive planning, such as for sewage and electrical utilities, was required before construction could begin. The land was cleared, and the state agriculture department was consulted about drainage ditches. It was important to build these ditches and a retention pond for water runoff. Extant city sewage lines were replaced by modern conveniences. Detroit Edison placed the electric lines underground to provide safety for the landing aircraft—electrical lines are difficult to see until a plane is practically on top of them. Because of all the special features, the cost of construction was to be closely monitored by other counties and cities involved in airport construction and by the aeronautical branch of the US Department of Commerce.

Soil samples were analyzed for sufficient uniformity in order to allow the drains to be laid out in straight lines across a field. Sixty-seven acres of land were covered with timber and had to be cleared. After accomplishing this, 17 miles of sewer were built at the field, and every drainage ditch was tested to make sure that the water would properly run off. When concrete runways were built, lights were installed on the outer edges of the length of the runway to ensure safe night landings. Colored lights were also installed, with green and red differentiating between runways.

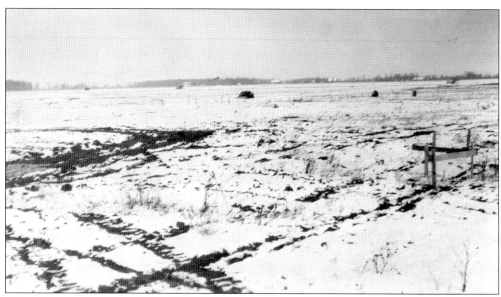

This is a winter view in 1928 of the Air National Guard building space before construction. Building in the winter is difficult because concrete does not set well in cold weather. (WHS.)

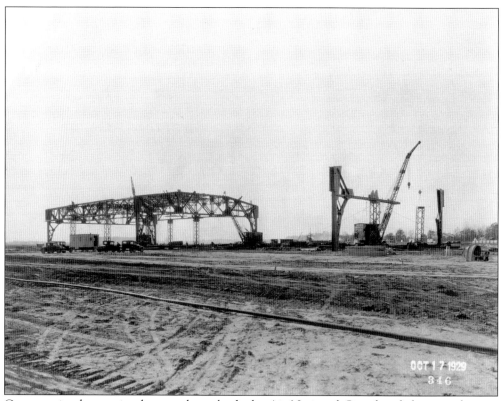

Construction began simultaneously on both the Air National Guard and the main hangar buildings. Even before it was completed, the landing field received incoming flights of airmail. (WHS.)

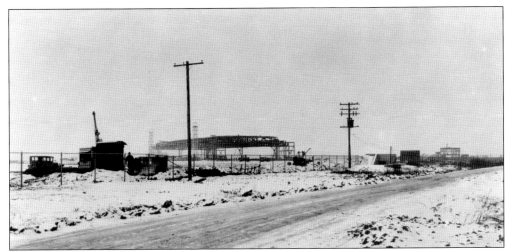

In this image from the winter of 1929, one can see the progress of both the hangar and the powerhouse (in the distance on the right). Since the airport had its own powerhouse, it was not dependent upon outside electricity. (WHS.)

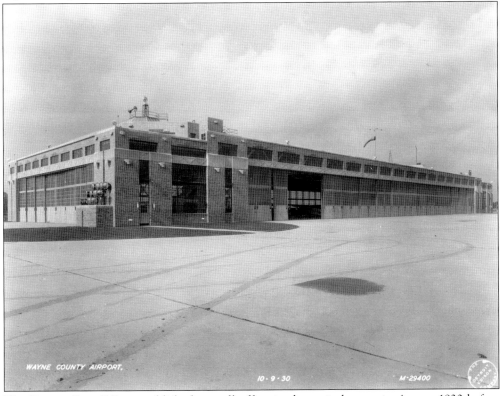

The Detroit Post Office established a small office in the main hangar in August 1930 before opening day. Other departments at Wayne County Airport included the US Weather Bureau, which had teletypes to deliver weather reports every hour from Chicago and Cleveland, and the engineering division of the aeronautical branch of the US Department of Commerce, which served as the place new pilots and mechanics came to for examinations and inspections of new aircraft built as far away as Wheeling, West Virginia. (WHS.)

Board of
County Road Commissioners
Wayne County

3800 BARLUM TOWER
Detroit, Michigan

August 25, 1930

Mrs. Eva Dugan
Romulus
Michigan

Dear Madam:-

      We hope you will be able to accept the invitation herein extended to you to be present at the dedication of the new Wayne County Airport on September 4, 1930.

      Thinking it might be interesting to some of the people who settled and have lived on the mile square which now harbors this Airport to fly over the property which was formerly theirs, we are asking you to be our guests on such a trip.

      If you have the desire for such an airplane ride, would you kindly notify either Mr. H. E. Baker at 3800 Barlum Tower, Detroit, Michigan, or, the Operations Officer at the Wayne County Airport, R.F.D.#2, Romulus, Michigan. If you can notify us by telephone, call Clifford 2333.

      On this flight an all metal trimotored Ford Plane will be used and it is available only on the day of the dedication, September 4th.

      Very sincerely yours

      BOARD OF COUNTY ROAD COMMISSIONERS

      Edward N. Hines

HEB*RH   Chairman
NON-TRANSFERABLE.
This letter must be presented by
you to obtain the ride.

ADDRESS ALL COMMUNICATIONS TO THE BOARD AND NOT TO INDIVIDUALS

This letter was sent to one of the people who lost property in the airport land acquisition. (RHS.)

Prior to the grand opening of the airport, Edward N. Hines, the president of the road commission board, offered airplane rides to some people who lived on the land on which the airport was built. Hines himself personally signed and sent out the letters. Anyone who received a letter simply had to call the operations officer at the airport; his phone number was in the letter. (WCDPS.)

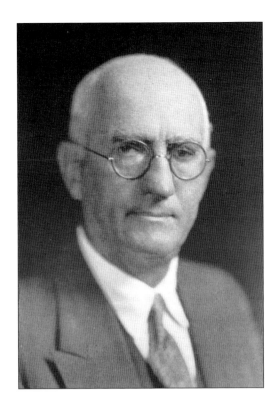

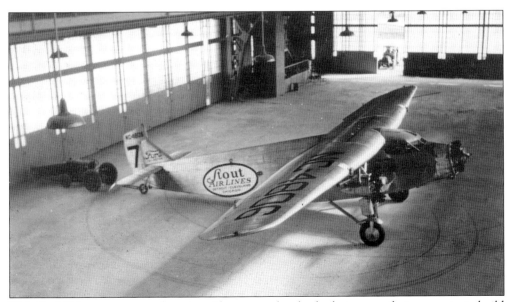

This Ford Tri-motor was used to give rides to people who had given up their property to build the airport. (WHS.)

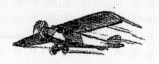

DEDICATION

OF THE

Wayne County Airport

INTERSECTION OF MIDDLE BELT AND GODDARD ROADS

at 2:00 O'Clock »» September 4th

« « « Nineteen Hundred Thirty » » »

You are cordially
invited to be present at the
informal dedication of Wayne
County's new Airport on the
above date and time.

Board of County Road Commissioners

EDWARD N. HINES, Chairman
JOHN S. HAGGERTY
WILLIAM F. BUTLER

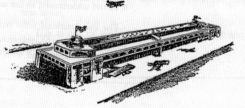

See Details on Page 2

On September 4, 1930, the day of the dedication of the Wayne County Airport, programs were handed out that explained what the local attendees' tax dollars paid for. Edward N. Hines gave a speech about the importance of this new airport. One inspiring statement still holds true today: "Huge transcontinental air liners will dock here; great freight carriers will zoom down from the sky; smaller craft of every description will follow the air lanes to this port. Passengers and freight will be speeded along the broad highways leading from this terminal to the metropolitan center. A great new industry will make this airport one of its important ports of call. This is not a dream of the future—it is an actuality of today." (RHS.)

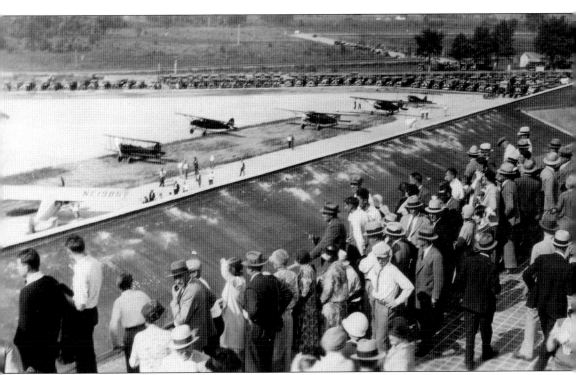

Wayne County hosted air shows throughout the 1930s that provided positive public relations and generated interest in potential passengers flying out of the airport. The turnout was never a problem; each year, people came to see what would be different. (WHS.)

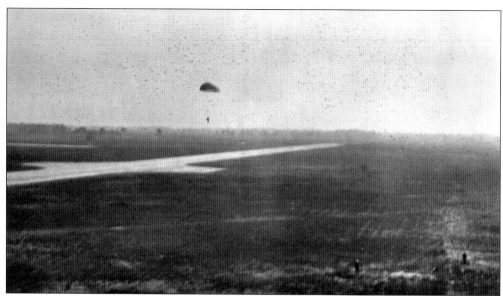

Of course, it would not be an air show without somebody doing something daring. This was the first parachute jump at the airport. The parachutist is unidentified, but it is certain that he or she certainly amazed the crowd. (WHS.)

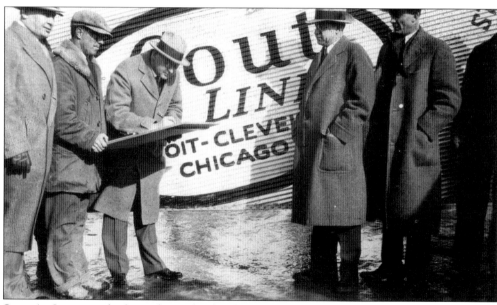

Stout Air Lines was the first airline to land at the airport. William Stout and Henry Ford partnered up to form the company in the mid-1920s, and they produced aircraft in Dearborn, Michigan. Eventually, Ford bought out Stout because he believed Stout did not have the ability to build and design quality aircraft. (WHS.)

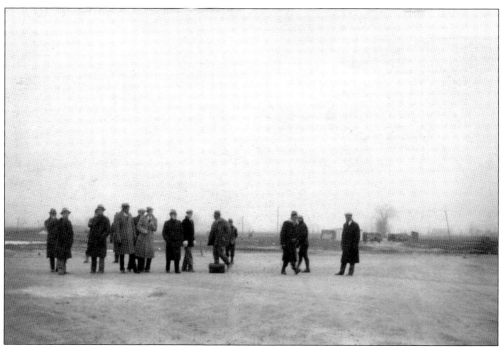

The first passengers gather to fly out of the airport. Their destination is unknown, as records for this flight have not been found; it was either Chicago or Cleveland, since those were the only places Stout Air Lines flew to at the time. (WHS.)

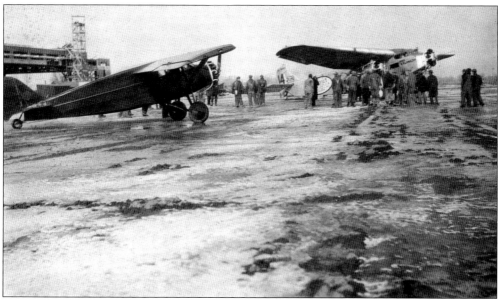

The airplane to the left was built by Stinson Aircraft Company in the city of Wayne, Michigan, just a few miles away. Stinson had a few factories in Michigan, and its planes were known to be reliable, tough flying machines. The British used them during World War II for observation and transport. To the right is a Ford Tri-motor. (WHS.)

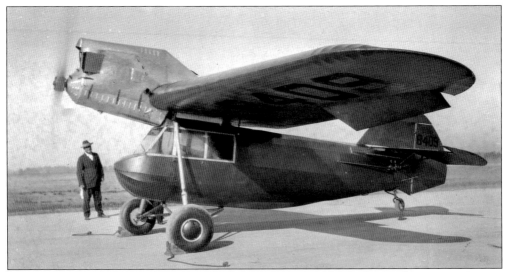

The aeronautical branch of US Department of Commerce had an office at the airport. Among the office's many tasks was the inspection of new prototype aircraft and approval of safety to fly them. This odd-looking plane, according to what was written on the photograph, was called the Taflang Beetle. It made its first flight at the grand opening of the airport. It is unknown how this plane flew, but apparently it did not have a very good landing, and the crowd was able to witness the airport's first airplane accident. (WHS.)

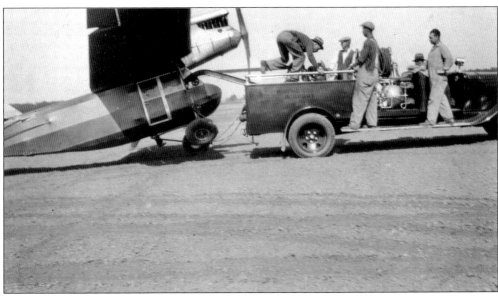

Besides performing building and ground maintenance, workers had to clean up plane wrecks. Later, they were trained to help put out fires during major crashes using the lone fire truck assigned to the airport. (WHS.)

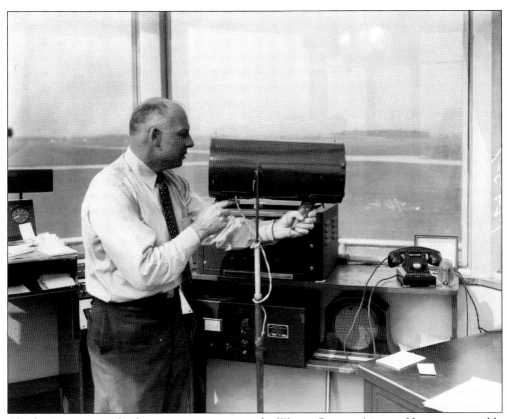

Charles Proctor was the first airport manager at the Wayne County Airport. He was responsible for overseeing operations of the airport, including building maintenance, landscaping, and flight control. Eventually, many of these duties were distributed to other personnel. (WHS.)

The control tower was the main base of operations at the airport. The taxiway and runway lighting was all operated there, so the airport manager could direct the pilots even if radio communication was lost or not established. (WHS.)

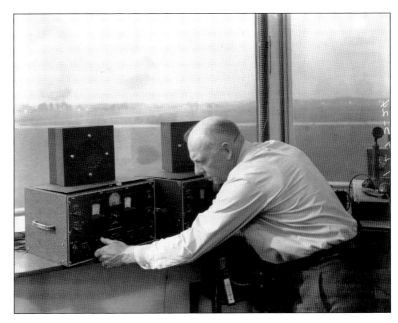

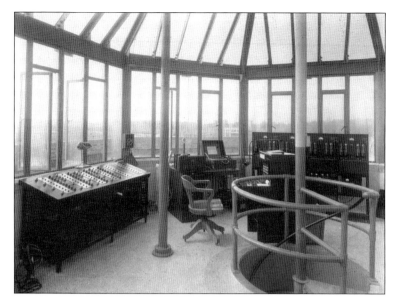

The south lookout tower in the main hangar contained the latest state-of-the-art equipment for tracking and communicating with aircraft. With plenty of sightlines and rooftop access, the air-traffic manager could follow aircraft on the ground as well in the air. (WHS.)

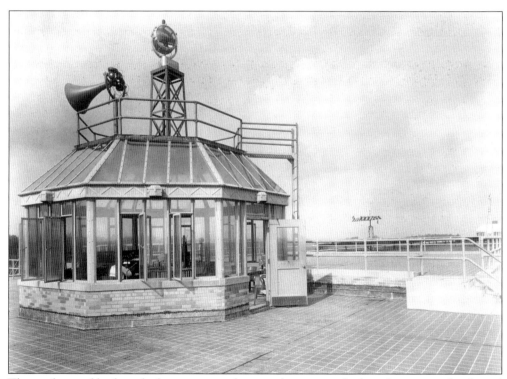

The roof around both outlook towers atop the main hangar was built with concrete, brick, and tile, with steel railings. When the tower was constructed, it was expected to be the center of airport operations. (WHS.)

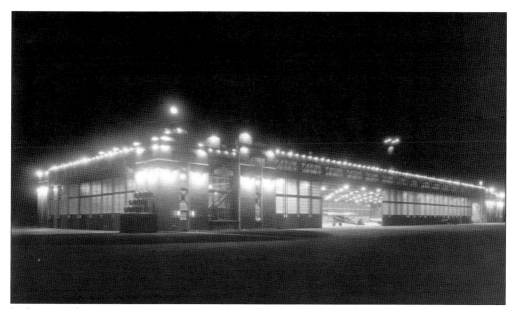

Lighting at the airport was very important, and the main hangar had plenty of it. This facility had enough illumination to be seen for miles on a clear night. The taxiways and runways had excellent lighting as well, which made Wayne County one the most advanced airports of its day. Below are some airmail carrier planes in the hangar; one was from Canada, and the others were from the US Department of Commerce. (WHS.)

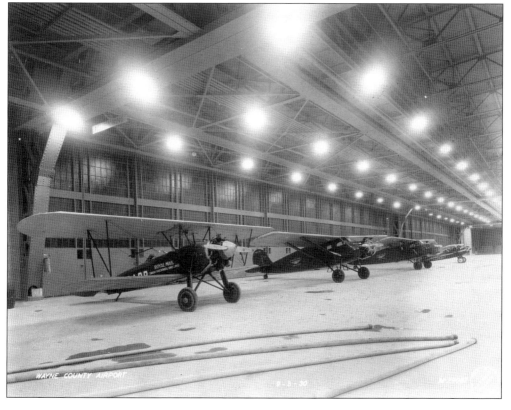

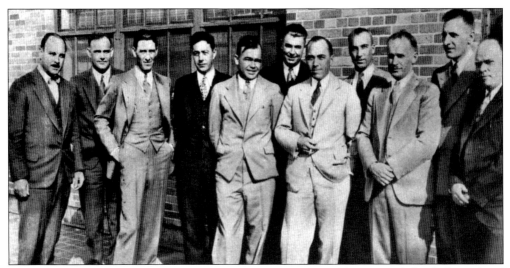

With the growth of air travel in the late 1930s, there was a need to control the flight paths of commercial and military air traffic. When the new airport terminal was completed in 1938, the aeronautical branch of the US Department of Commerce hired these men as the official air-traffic agents of Wayne County Airport. (WCAA.)

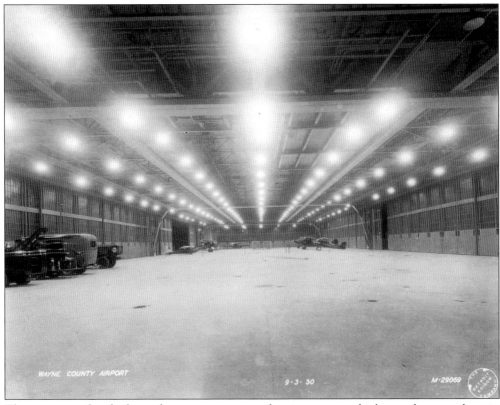

There was no other facility to house emergency and maintenance vehicles, so they were kept in the main hangar throughout the 1930s. In this 1930 image, the vehicles to the left and planes in the background give good perspective of the size of the hangar. (WHS.)

The US Weather Bureau operated out of the observation tower on the north side of the hangar. The wind sock determined the direction of the wind, and other equipment was also placed on the roof to gather readings. "Wayne County Airport" was spelled out in large letters on the roof so pilots could see them from the sky. In the 1930s, flying was done visually, as radar and modern electronics did not yet exist. (WHS.)

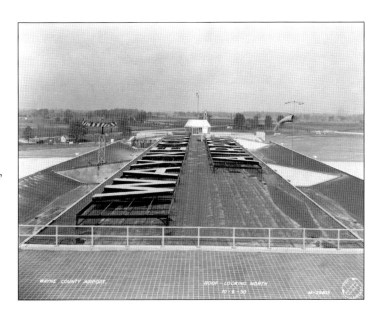

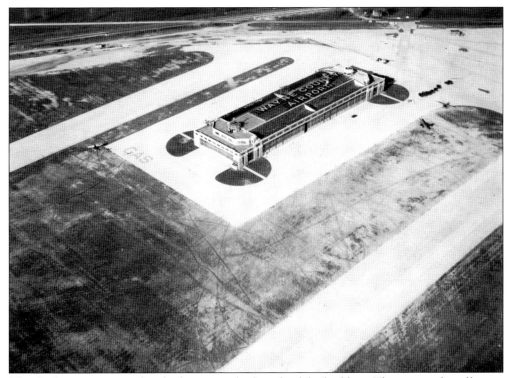

This facility was equipped with elevators at both ends of the building. There were also offices at both ends of the building, while the south side had a public lounge and showers and restrooms for workers and pilots. The north side contained a parachute-packing room and a parachute-drying room. The radio room was on the second floor. (WHS.)

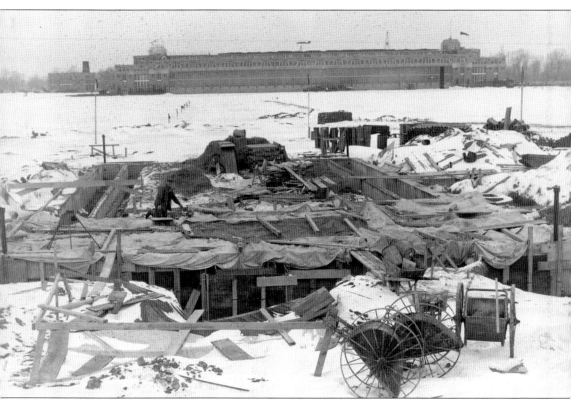

Upon realizing that people were becoming comfortable with the thought of flying instead of taking the train, the county invested in a new air terminal. Construction started in 1937 and was completed a year later. Wayne County Executive Terminal boasted features that other airports did not have at the time, including a barbershop, a restaurant, a ticket counter, a post office, and a telegraph office on the first floor. The second floor housed the Civil Aeronautics Authority (CAA), and there was a new, modern control tower at the top of the building. (WHS.)

The Executive Terminal provided a central point for passengers catching flights. With its Art Deco interior and exterior, Wayne County Airport advertised the fact that it had all the modern conveniences. (WCAA.)

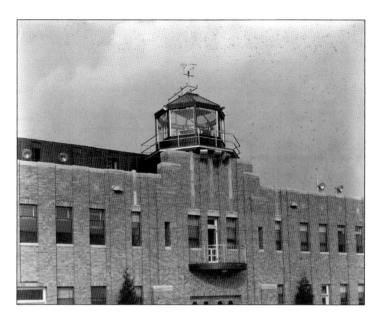

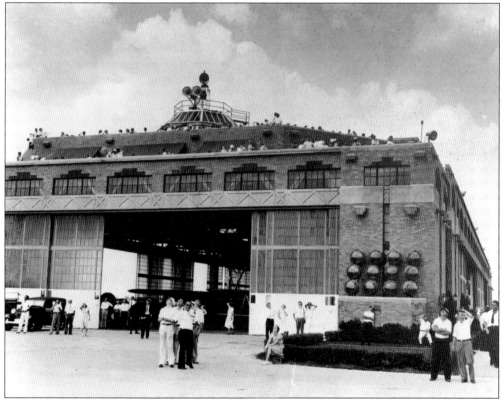

The open-house air shows at the airport were discontinued at the end of the 1930s. This was how the hangar looked in 1939 before the Army Corps of Engineers (ACE) modified it. The US Army Air Corps leased the airport from 1941 to 1946. Later, the Wayne County Road Commission made plans for expansion of the airport, and by 1951 the airport hosted the National Air Races. (WHS.)

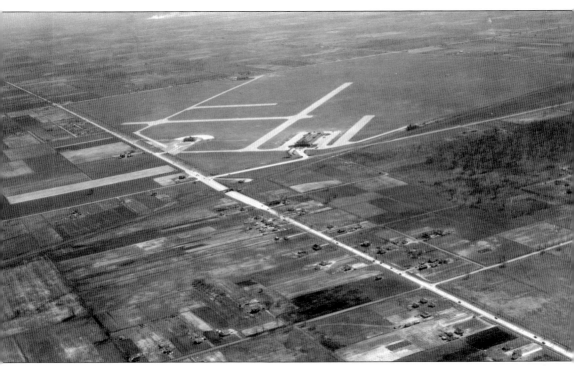

This aerial view shows Wayne County Airport in 1938 after the Executive Terminal was erected. It went through more changes during the 1940s when the US Army Air Corps leased the entire airport in 1941. The Executive Terminal, which served as an administration building, had additions built by the Army Corps of Engineers, and property east of Middlebelt Road was procured for housing and other structures necessary for a military base. (WHS.)

Two

ROMULUS ARMY AIRFIELD

In 1941, the US Army realized that it needed air bases throughout the United States in order to shuttle bombers and fighter planes. The Civilian Pilot Training Program and a variety of other miscellaneous activities helped make Wayne County Airport the fourth-busiest airport in the country. A peak 1,800 flights per day made it an excellent base of operations for the US Army Air Corps Ferry Command. The US War Department leased half the airfield and the main hangar. Many previous improvements to the airport saved the government money, but there was still a need for more facilities. The Air National Guard hangar was doubled in area, and new structures included barracks, administration buildings, hangars, and recreation facilities.

Some civilian personnel were kept in place for maintenance, and civilian pilots helped train new pilots. By the summer of 1941, the whole airport was controlled by the US War Department. The airport was designated the Romulus Army Airfield and handled by the 345th Air Transport Command. The airport also became home for the 3rd Ferrying Group, and the 107th Observation Group was reassigned to another base.

By 1942, Henry Ford had a bomber plant up and running; some pilots flew the B-24 Liberator bomber to different areas of the United States. Light aircraft built in Michigan (not from Willow Run) were transported from Romulus, and other aircraft were brought to the airport from other states. At Romulus, they were refueled and inspected and eventually transported to the East Coast.

British pilots learning to fly at Naval Air Station Grosse Ile would encounter the Army flying B-24s south along the railroad tracks from Detroit to Toledo. The Army would fly low enough to create rough turbulence for the training pilots in their Stearman biplane trainers.

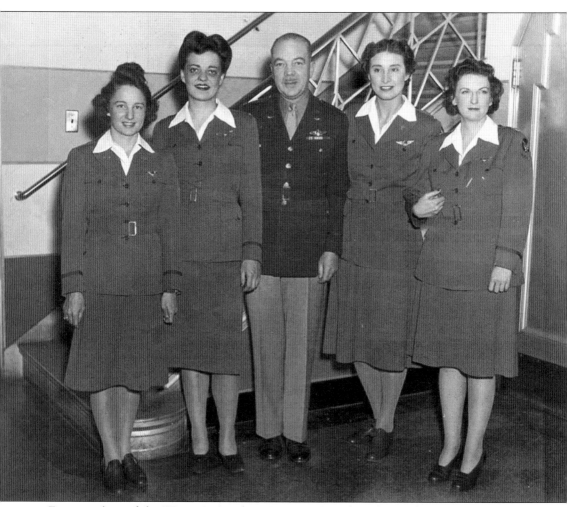

Four members of the Women's Auxiliary Ferrying Squadron (WAFS) are pictured with base commander Col. Carlyle Nelson in January 1943. Shown here are, from left to right, Katherine Rawls Thompson, Barbara Donahue, Colonel Nelson, Adela Riek Scharr, and Barbara Poole. Between January 1943 and December 1944, one hundred or so female ferry pilots (later known as the Women Airforce Service Pilots, or WASP) joined the male ferry pilots assigned to Romulus. When the war started, Scharr's husband joined the service, and she was approached to join the newly formed WAFS. A former teacher who became interested in flying, Scharr was appointed group leader of the WAFS in Romulus. She and Donahue trained together and became accomplished pursuit pilots. Scharr was transferred to another base to fly advanced pursuit planes like the P-51 Mustang. (SLPL.)

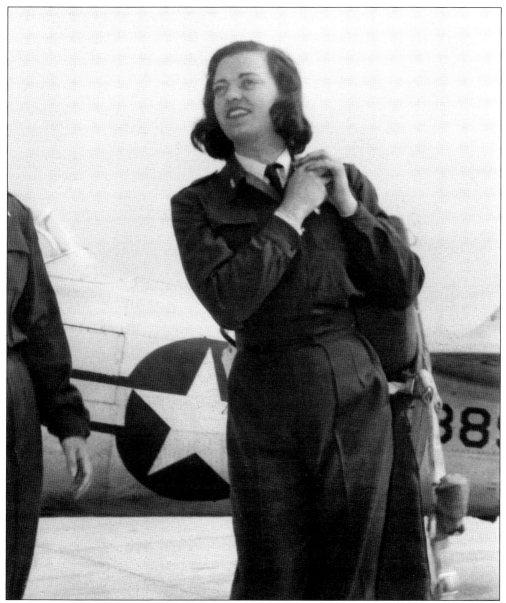

After Adela Scharr was transferred to another base, Barbara Donahue became the group leader for the WAFS at Romulus. She had the respect of the other pilots with the skills she attained. Donahue liked to talk about the time she landed a P-39 Airacobra on a road someplace along the northern route to Great Falls, a tale included in *The Originals*, Sarah B. Rickman's book about the WAFS. Donahue's airplane developed a problem that could only be fixed on the ground. Looking for a good place to land, she spotted what appeared to be a deserted highway. As she was making her final approach, she flew over a bus. People on the bus were quite surprised when an airplane with a large red star on the fuselage landed right in front of them and a female pilot climbed out. The bus driver asked, "What's the matter, lady? Get tired of flying?" Since she was blocking his path, he had to wait for her to make the necessary repairs. The driver did not lend a hand and instead became agitated when he realized he was falling behind schedule. As soon as the repairs were made, Donahue waved good-bye and took off. (TWU.)

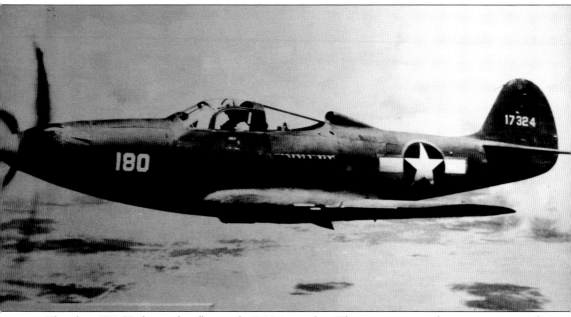

The plane WASPs learned to fly was the P-39 Airacobra. The nose contained a cannon mounted with two 50-caliber machine guns. The plane had tricycle landing gear, which helped pilots during takeoff as it allowed them to see the runway more clearly. The drawback was that if the nose gear collapsed on takeoff or landing, the force of the engine behind the cockpit would crush the pilot in a crash. Another problem was that the cockpit had doors instead of a retractable canopy—if a pilot had to bail out of a plane, it would be difficult to open the door at speed. An experienced P-39 pilot explained that it did not take turns very well either. The US Army did not have much use for the plane except for training, so the P-39s were sold to the Soviet Union to be used for close ground support. (TANHM.)

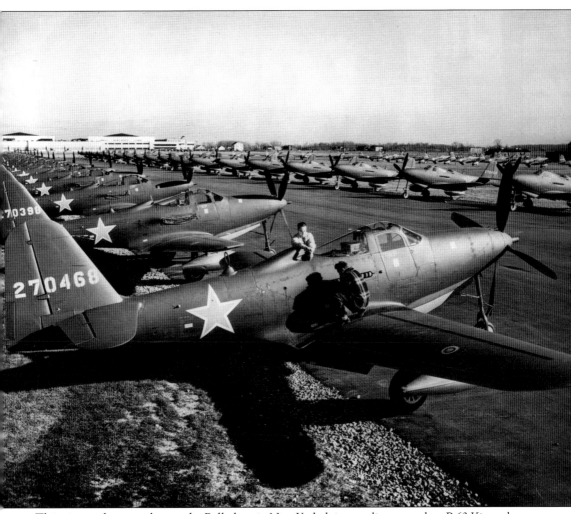

This picture shows workers at the Bell plant in New York doing quality control on P-63 Kingcobras, a slightly larger version of the P-39. The fuselage has been extended, the cockpit moved forward, and the engine, although still behind the pilot, has been moved forward as well to allow the plane to have more fuel capacity and armament. Even with the adjustments, the plane still had the same faults as the P-39. An additional problem created was that the P-63 was prone to overheating when taking off too fast. It also had doors instead of an opening canopy and a stationary nose gear that did not turn left or right while taxiing. The plane also arrived too late in the war to have been of any help for the allies except for the Russians, who used them for close ground support and as tank destroyers. (BAM.)

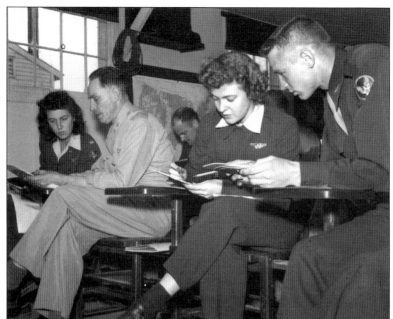

One of the primary functions of Romulus was the training of new pilots as well as the training of experienced pilots on new aircraft flown out of the base. Men and women trained together to learn the specifics of aircraft that were to be transported across the United States. (TWU.)

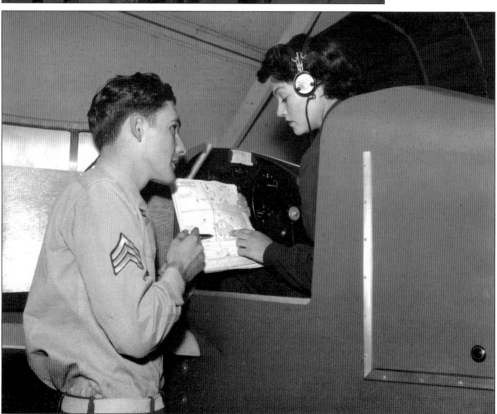

Margaret Ann (Hamilton) Tunner receives instructions of what to do inside this early flight simulator known as a Link Trainer, which was used to help new pilots learn about night flying with instruments only. (TWU.)

All Army Air Forces bases had parachute-packing buildings, and Romulus was no exception. Here, pilots Marjorie Logan (left) and Joanne Trebtoske pick up parachutes for their next assignment. (TWU.)

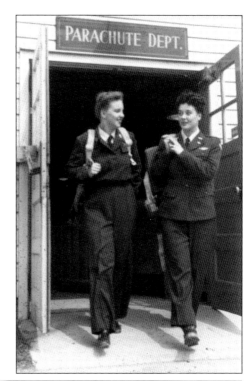

The building was situated across from the Air National Guard hangar. It was used for packing parachutes, as well as to inspect them for rips and holes, so the life-saving equipment would perform without fail if a problem occurred during flight. (SMAM.)

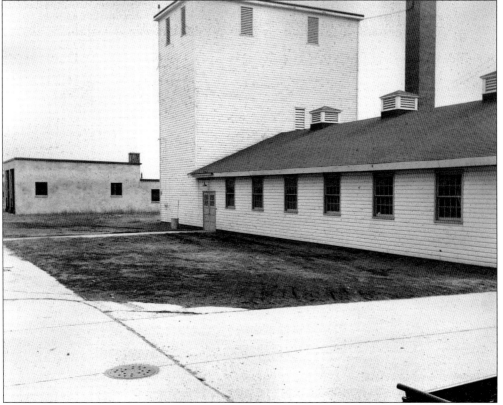

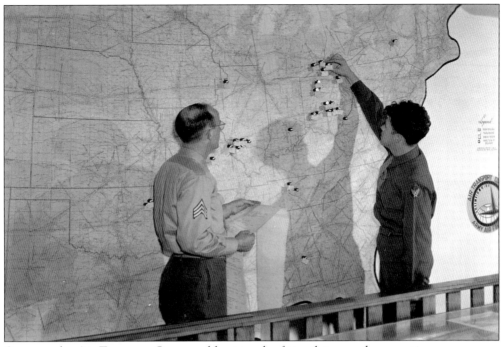

One way the Air Transport Command kept track of its pilots was the operations map room. Here, at Romulus, two servicemen plot a pilot's location on the map. At right, the Air Transport Command insignia is visible on the wall. (SMAM.)

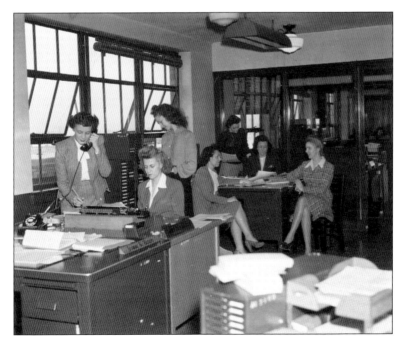

Civilian personnel were essential in performing office duties on the base since many official personnel were overseas fighting the war. Women handled much of the office work. (SMAM.)

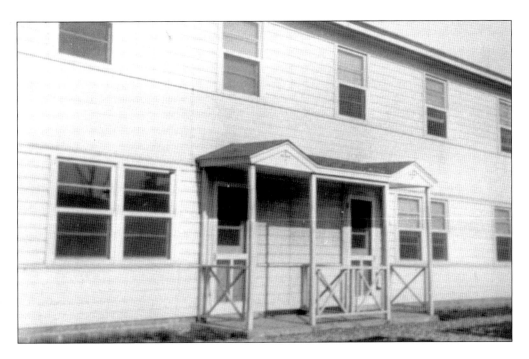

The building above was one of the facilities that housed female pilots. The first female pilots' residence was only a one-story building. According to the Army Corps of Engineers blueprint, the structure below was originally a mess hall but later became the operations building for the WASP. Commander Barbara Donahue and executive officer Lenore McElroy had offices in the building, and the female pilots reported there every day for assignments. These buildings were recently razed in 2009. (TWU.)

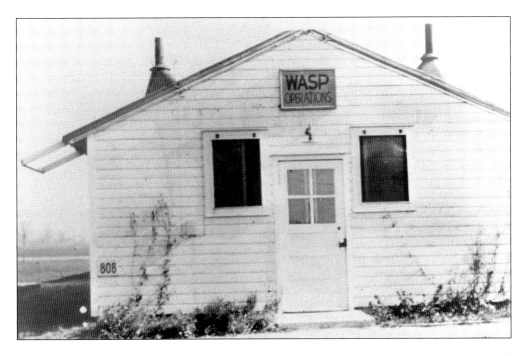

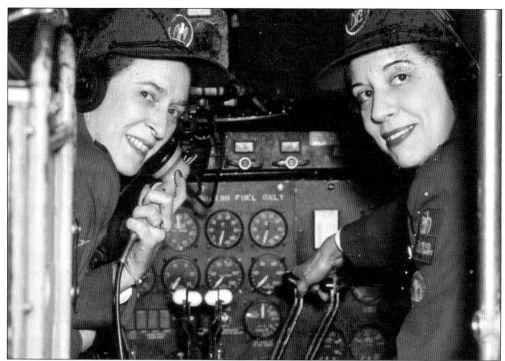

Above, two members of the American Women's Voluntary Services are sitting in the cockpit of a C54D Skymaster. Below, a few volunteers gather around the coffee shop on the base. The base provided relaxing activities for both men and women, but there was bus service to nearby towns so personnel could go see a movie or take in a meal at a local diner. (SMAM.)

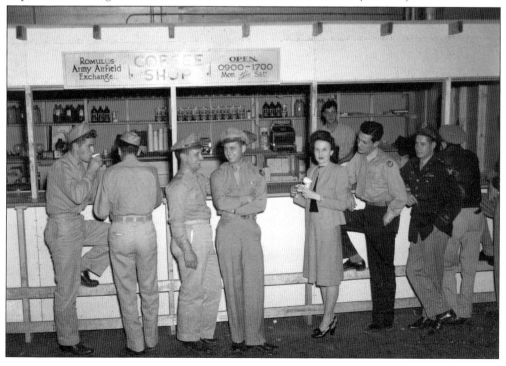

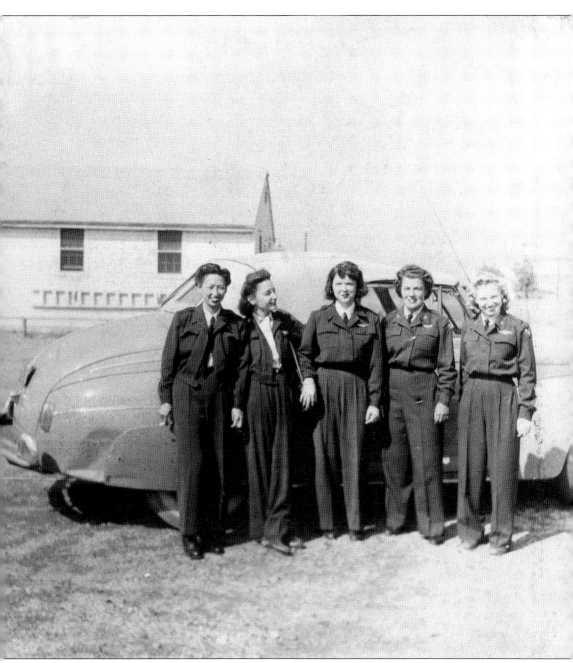

Five of the pilots stationed with the 3rd Ferrying Group in Romulus are pictured here. From left to right they are Hazel Ah Ying Lee, Alice Jean Starr, Virginia Hagerstrom, Alice Lovejoy, and Sylvia Clayton. Lee was one of two Chinese-American women to serve with the WASP during World War II. Thirty-eight WASPs died in service during the war—Lee and Lovejoy were two of them. Lee was the victim of an air-traffic control error as she prepared to land at Great Falls, Montana, on November 23, 1944. Her P-63 collided with another airplane and burst into flames. Dragged alive from the wreckage, she died two days later as a result of her burns. Lovejoy died on September 13, 1944, in a training accident at Pursuit School in Brownsville, Texas. (TWU.)

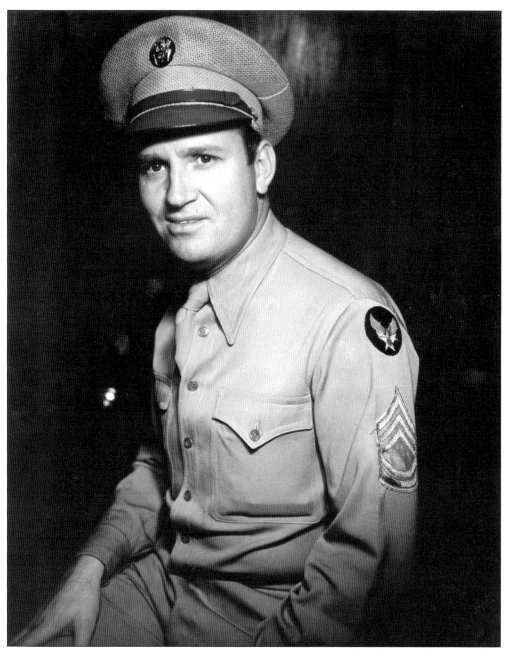

Gene Autry, known as the "Singing Cowboy," was stationed at Romulus in 1945. He had served a tour of duty in China and returned to the United States to ferry and fly cargo. Autry joined the Army Air Forces when he was refused enlistment by the other branches of the armed forces because of his age. He held the rank of flight officer and was well respected by his peers. While in the service, he still did his show on Armed Forces Radio, and after returning to the United States he did war-bond drives across the country. (USAF.)

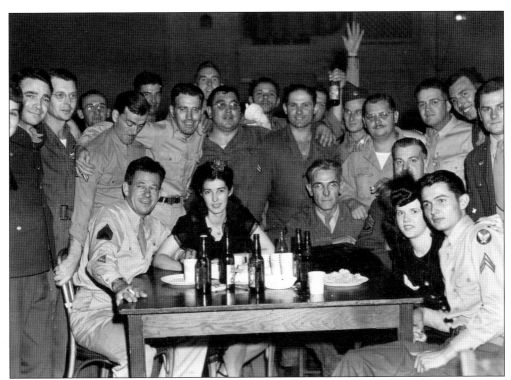

This group celebrates the end of the war at a farewell party in September 1945. By 1946, control of the airport began to return to Wayne County. Many of the jobs at the airport reverted to civilian personnel. By 1947, Wayne County was back in complete control of the airport. (SMAM.)

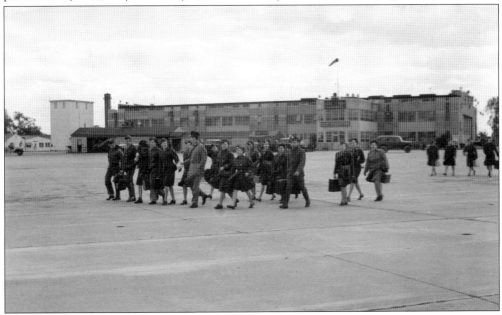

Servicemen and women were discharged in October 1945. In the background is the original Air National Guard building, erected in 1929, with the parachute-packing building to the left. (SMAM.)

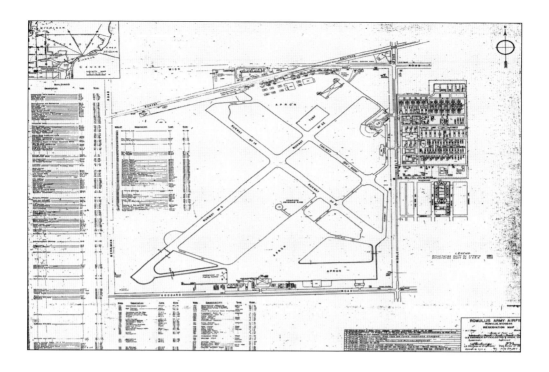

When it built around the airport, the Army Corps of Engineers assigned numbers to all the structures. When the ACE laid out the blueprints, the key had the numbers of the structures and listed what they were. After the airport was built, the county used this numbering system for all new structures. Below, a key shows closer view system with numbers, structures, and sizes. (RHS.)

340	Reclamation Shed		RECL-4-A	20 x 50
271				
272	B.D. Inspection		Wood	20 x 88
278	North Hangar		Brick	125 x 434
279	Air Freight Terminal		Wood	40 x 95
280				
281	Lavatory		L-F-T	20 x 104
282	Gasoline Control - Aircraft Fueling Shed		Brick	8 x 10
283				
284	Skeet Range			
347A	Flag Pole			
348	Administration Bldg		Brick	45 x 100
352	Transformer Vault		Brick	14.3 x 19
451	Link Trainer Bldg		SH.9 Mod	24 x 116

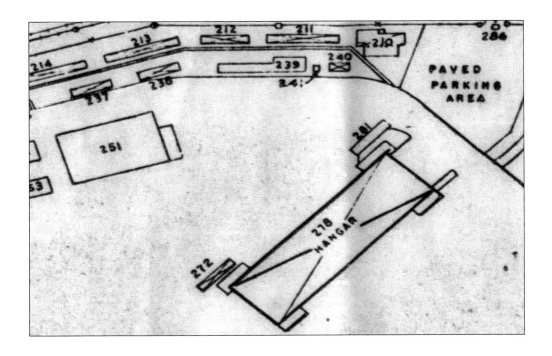

The original hangar that opened in 1930 was assigned a number (278) that is still used today. In the photograph below, taken in the early 1950s, one can see the modifications the military made to the original hangar. These additional structures were torn down in the 1980s, and the main hangar was put into use as a maintenance facility. (Above, WCAA; below, WHS.)

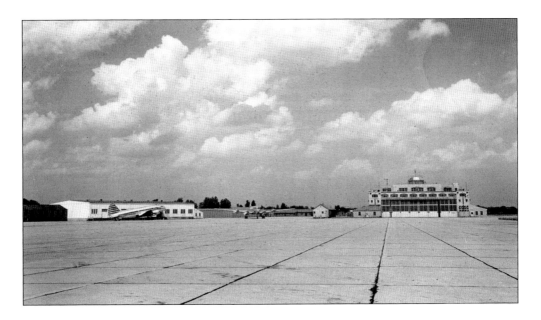

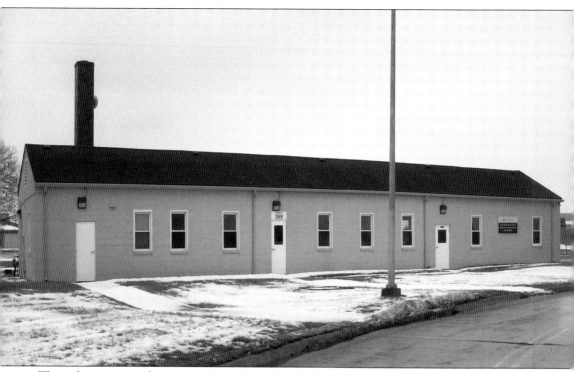

The only structures that remain from the military era are buildings 349 and 352. Building 352 is a transformer vault, and 349 (shown here) was a telephone and telegraph facility but is now a utility facility. (Author's collection.)

Three

DETROIT-WAYNE MAJOR AIRPORT

By 1946, even before it regained control from the military, Wayne County had approved the expansion of the airport. The county considered the military improvements inadequate and even thought they were damaging to the civilian functions at the airport.

The newer airport terminals were named after people associated with its growth. The L.C. Smith Terminal, constructed in 1957, was named after the man who was there from the beginning as the airport's master architect and who eventually became Wayne County chairman. The Davey Terminal, built in 1966, was named so in 1975 for the airport's assistant manager who served from the late 1950s. The Berry Terminal, constructed in 1974, was named for Michael Berry, a former airport commissioner. Eventually, in 2002, the newly built south terminal replaced the Davey Terminal; it was named for Edward H. McNamara, the former Wayne County executive.

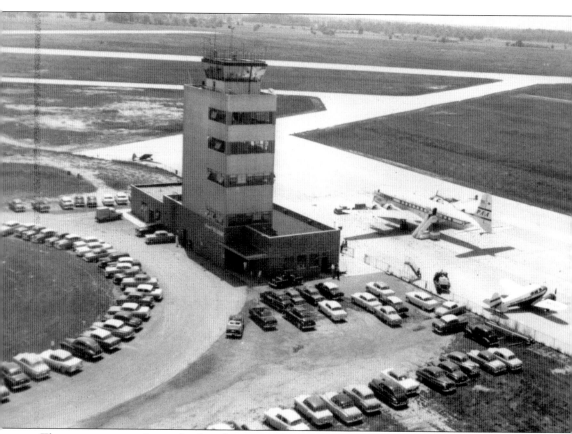

The county acquired more land to the west and south of the original airport in order to expand, bringing the area up to a total of four square miles—$4.5 million had been allocated to expand and upgrade the airport. (WCAA.)

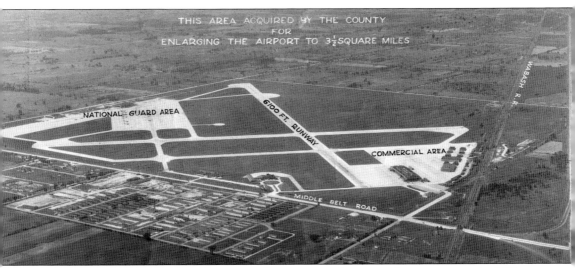

The county built more runways, hangars, and a new control tower and passenger terminal. The plan was to relieve the amount of cargo flights out of Willow Run Airport and passenger flights from Detroit City Airport. (WCAA.)

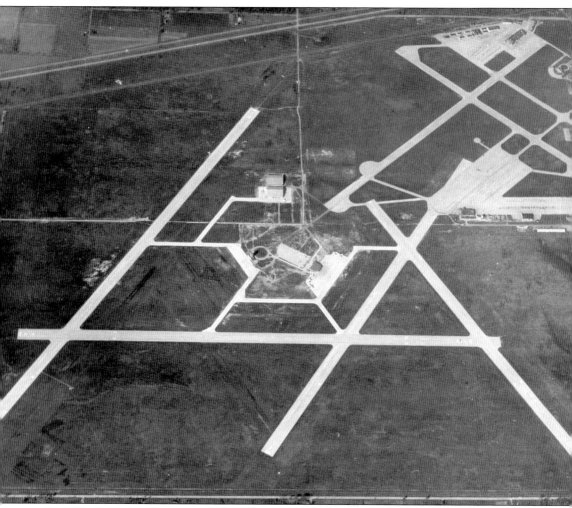

By 1951, the airport had expanded to what can be seen in this aerial photograph. The original landing strip used by the Army is in the upper right corner; the new airstrip is visible in the rest of the photograph, including three runways: two running southwest and one running west to east. For a short time, the National Guard was stationed at Luke Airfield. The county leased the vacant facilities until it returned. In the meantime, the county planned to make Detroit-Wayne Major Airport the best in the United States. With Interstate 94 stretching from Willow Run Airport past Detroit-Wayne Major and into Detroit, it was obvious the airport was the right investment for further expansion and to modernize facilities. There was plenty of room to let the airport grow since most of the surrounding properties were farmland. The buildings left behind by the military were utilized for small businesses and as housing for World War II veterans and men at the Air National Guard and Nike bases. (WHS.)

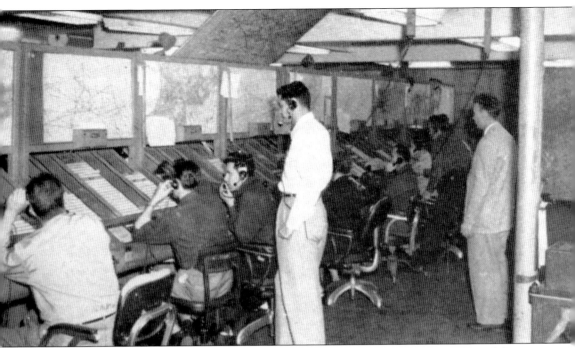

Even though the military had radar, the Civil Aeronautics Authority at Detroit-Wayne Major did not have the capabilities. A team of men kept track of the inbound and outbound flights using cards and slots. Pilots called their locations in to air-traffic control, and when they reached a certain position they were passed off to the next CAA representative. Eventually, the federal government upgraded the airport with radar in 1956. (WCDPS.)

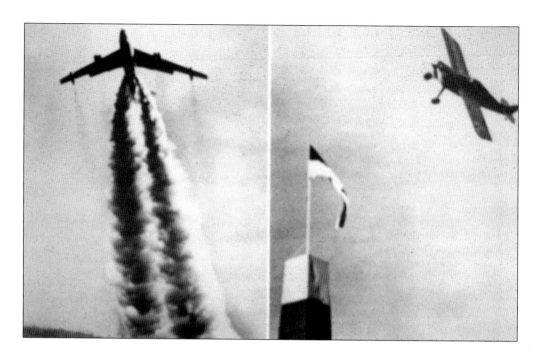

Since its grand opening in 1930, the airport had been a venue for open-house events in which the public is invited to check out different types of aircraft. The events included air races, flight demonstrations, and precision flying from the armed forces' special flying teams such as the Blue Angels. The open houses served to attract locals to the airport and as positive public relations. During World War II, the open houses went on hiatus, but after the war they continued for a time as Aero Club of Michigan International Aviation Expositions. (WCDPS.)

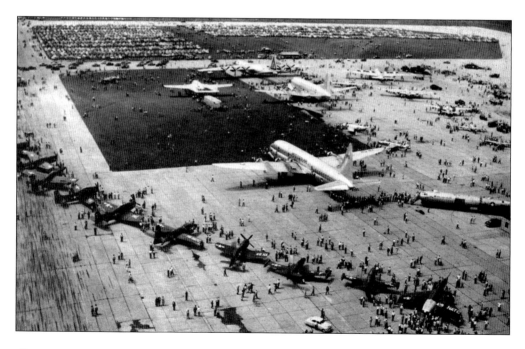

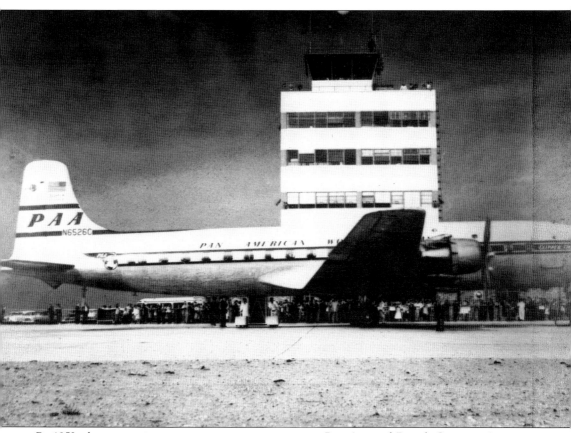

By 1952, the two major passenger service carriers were Pan Am and British Overseas Airways, which conducted international flights. Eventually, additional larger passenger services moved from Willow Run to Detroit-Wayne Major Airport. This relieved the amount of air traffic at Willow Run and helped to avoid delays of regularly scheduled flights. (WHS.)

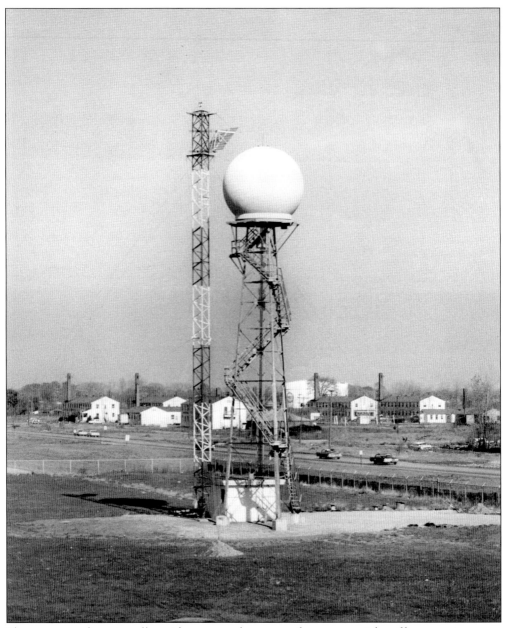

Plans were made to install a wide-range radar system for commercial traffic, meaning more employment and more flights to Detroit as more commercial jetliners flew into Detroit-Wayne Major. The Civil Aeronautics Authority increased employment by at least 27 people and continued round-the-clock monitoring of flights in the area. A weather radar tower is pictured here. The tower, sans the white sphere, still stands today next to the airport police building. (WCAA.)

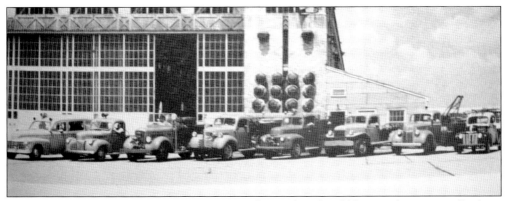

Maintenance and emergency equipment was still stored in the old hangar, but eventually those vehicles moved to a facility closer to the new runways. No one had a designated position or specialty job at the time, and all personnel were trained to work with both the fire and snow-removal equipment. (WCDPS.)

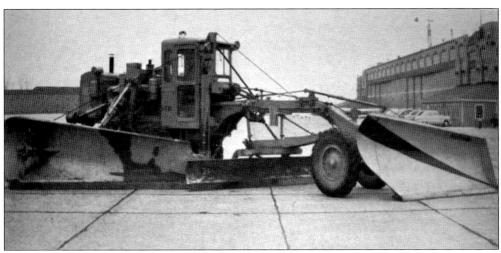

During the winter months, the runways and aprons were constantly cleared to ensure timely departures and arrivals of all flights. State-of-the-art snowplows at the time handled heavy snowfalls. (WCDPS.)

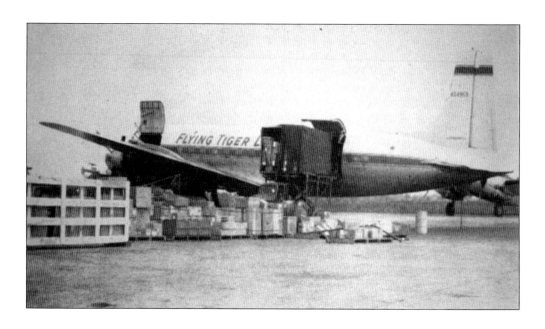

In the early 1950s, Slick Airways and Flying Tiger were the largest air-cargo carriers flying out of Detroit-Wayne Major. Slick Airways disappeared, and other carriers like Meteor and Zantop started operations there. Flying Tiger moved pilot operations to Detroit-Wayne Major in the mid-1950s and kept a presence there until the 1980s, when Federal Express took over its operations. (WCDPS.)

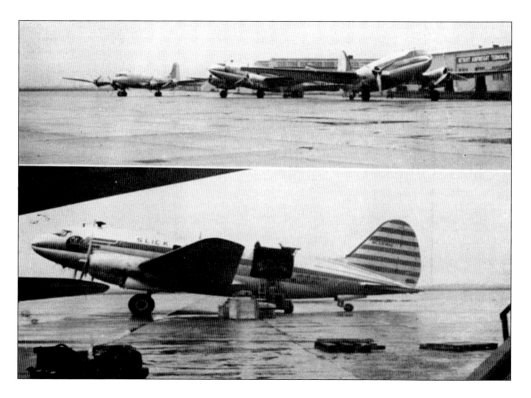

Four

MICHIGAN AIR NATIONAL GUARD

The 107th Observation Squadron was formed in Michigan in 1926 as part of the 32nd Division of the Michigan National Guard. The guard was based in River Rouge until 1931, when it moved its base of operations to the Wayne County Airport. The headquarters were located on Goddard Road and served as a hangar as well as housing offices. By 1940, the US Army Air Corps had leased part of the airport and started making changes, including expanding the Air National Guard hangar. Just before World War II, an addition was made to the east side of the building that doubled the facility's size.

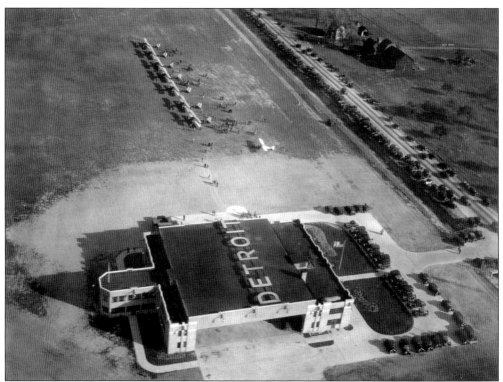

The 107th Observation Squadron was equipped with Consolidated PT-1s. Pilots may have used the runway to takeoff with these aircraft, but they most likely landed on the grass or used the grass to slow down. The old biplanes did not have brakes, and since they were "tail draggers," it was difficult to control steering on pavement. During air shows, crowds were still pleased to see the guard fly these aircraft. The unit used the planes throughout the 1930s, eventually receiving newer aircraft as war broke out in Europe that included Douglas BT-1s, O-2s, and O-38s and North American O-47s and BC-2s. (The O represents "observation" and the P stands for "pursuit," thus the O-47 is not to be confused with the Republic P-47, for example.) (Above, WHS; below, WHS.)

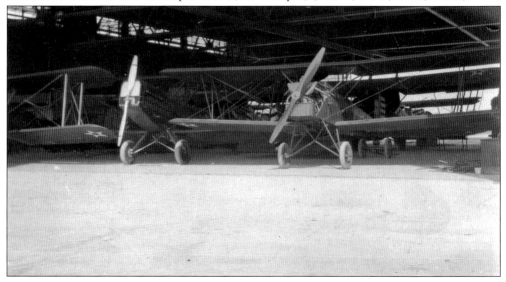

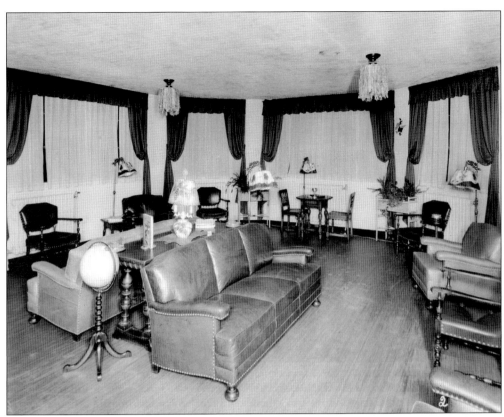

The National Guard building, with its front facing south, was constructed in 1930 as a hangar with offices. The first-floor south building held offices, a first-aid room, a stock room, and a photographic workroom. On the second floor were two bedrooms and two classrooms. In between the north and south parts of the building was the hangar, where planes were stored or worked on. The north part faced the airfield, and its first floor held an engineering and overhaul shop, bedrooms, and an observation room. The second floor contained a parachute-packing room, locker room, kitchen, dining room, and an officers' club. (SMAM.)

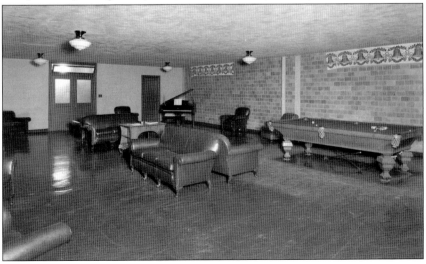

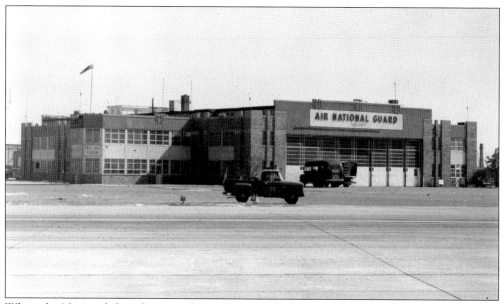

When the National Guard returned, it still occupied the east side of the airport at Middlebelt and Goddard Roads where Goddard entered the airport property. A Nike missile base was erected south of Goddard Road, with housing, administration, and operations buildings. (SMAM.)

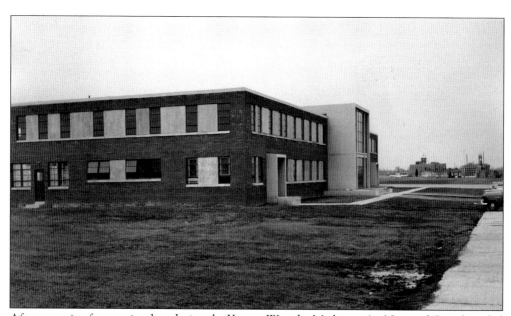

After returning from active duty during the Korean War, the Michigan Air National Guard needed a larger headquarters; the 127 Tactical Reconnaissance Wing was stationed at Romulus from 1952 to 1971. Today the headquarters is being utilized by Metro Airport Police. (SMAM.)

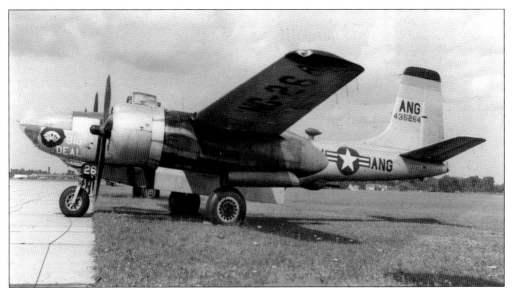

This Douglas B-26 Invader is pictured during World War II as an Air National Guard plane, the A-26. When aircraft are transferred from the Air Force to Air National Guard, the markings on them are changed; the "ANG" on the tail of this plane denotes "Air National Guard." The A-26 was the first new aircraft assigned to the 107th after World War II, even though it had already been used during the war and seen combat. (SMAM.)

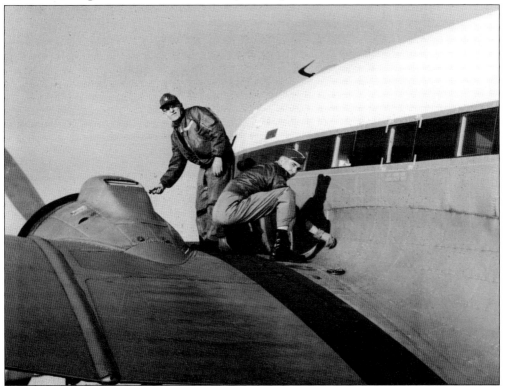

The flight crew of this C-47 Skytrain is doing the all-important aircraft inspection before takeoff to minimize the possibility of malfunction while in flight. (SMAM.)

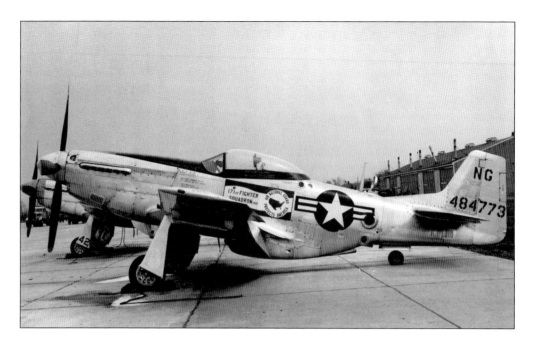

By 1948, the Army Air Corps was an independent branch of the armed forces that was evolving into the US Air Force. At this time, the markings changed from National Guard (NG) to Air National Guard (ANG). The markings for planes changed as well: the P-51 Mustang was designated as F-51 with the F representing "fighter." The plane above has National Guard markings, and it is dressed for air shows with a fitted observation camera located just behind the star insignia. When aircraft from the Air Force or other National Guard units outside of Michigan are transferred to Michigan, the markings are changed, as seen below on the fuselage and tail of this F-51. The F-51 replaced the A-26 to prepare the wing for jets. (SMAM.)

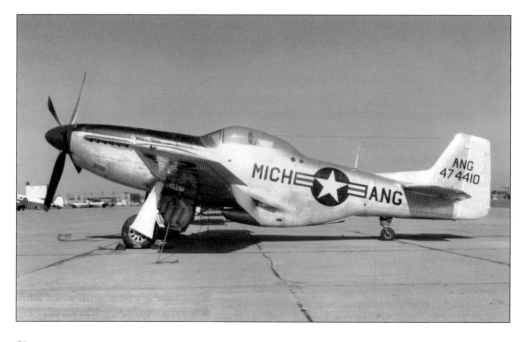

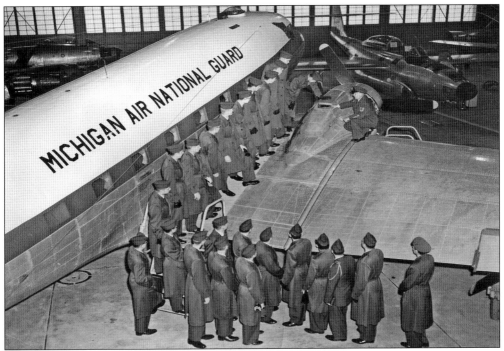

M.Sgt. Anthony Sallenger explains how the engine operates on the C-47 to a group of junior Air Force Reserve Officer Training Corps cadets. Since the governor of Michigan was commander in chief of the National Guard and Air National Guard of Michigan, he had use of this particular C-47 quite often. (SMAM.)

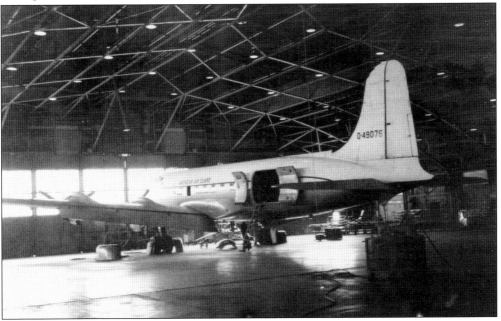

This C-54 Skymaster, used in the Berlin Airlift, arrived at Romulus with coal dust in the cargo hold. Like most of the planes the Air National Guard received, it was well used and needed repairs and cleaning. (SMAM.)

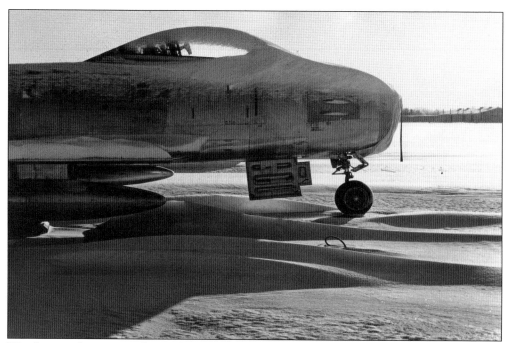

Weather conditions are always changing in Michigan; here, an F-86 Sabre is exposed to the harsh winter of the Great Lakes state. There was never enough hangar space to protect all the aircraft from the elements, but other precautions were taken. In this photograph, the intakes on the engine are covered to prevent ice and snow buildup. (SMAM.)

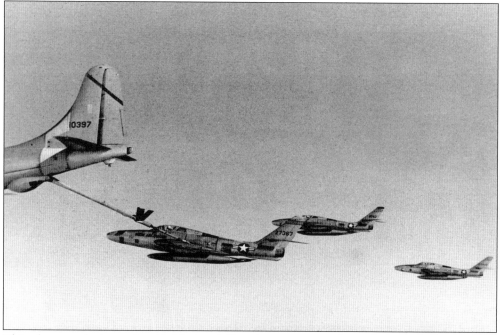

This photograph shows the Air National Guard practicing midair refueling—a necessity for long flights and missions. A Boeing KC-97 Stratotanker is shown refueling Republic RF-84F Thunderflashes of the 127th Tactical Reconnaissance Wing. (SMAM.)

Capt. Arnold G. Wackerman (left), from the 107th Fighter Interceptor Wing of the New York Air Guard, is shown with actress Anne Francis and Gen. Winston Wilson after Wackerman took second place in the 1955 Ricks Memorial Trophy Race. The cross-country competition that year started in Ontario, California, and ended at Detroit-Wayne Major. The race was named for Maj. Gen. Earl T. Ricks. (SMAM.)

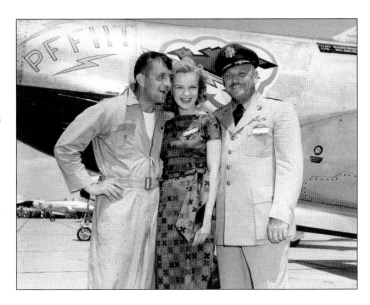

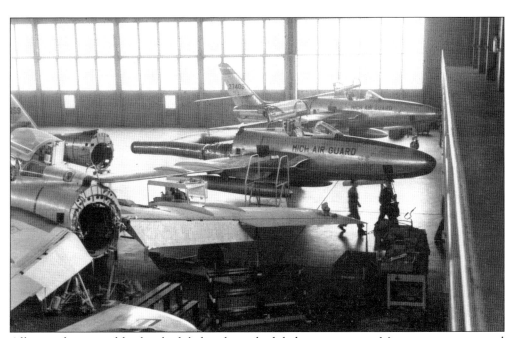

All aircraft required both scheduled and unscheduled maintenance. Maintenance personnel basically overhauled the entire aircraft, repairing and/or replacing jet engines, radios, navigational aids, instruments, and aerial reconnaissance cameras. (SMAM.)

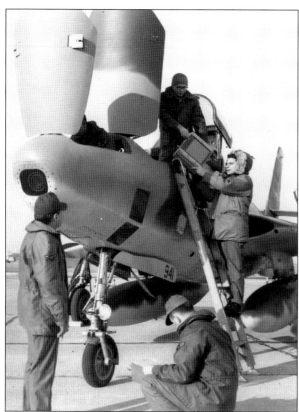

In this image, Air National Guardsmen remove the film from an RF-84F Thunderflash after a mission. The nose camera and camera windows on the side and bottom of the aircraft are visible. (SMAM.)

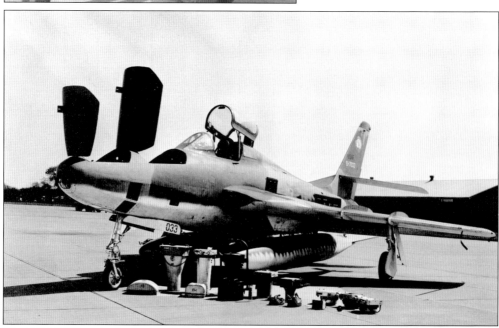

The RF-84F Thunderflash, shown here along with camera equipment spread out on the tarmac, contained six cameras with different lenses for various views and angles of targets. The cameras were placed in the two compartments in the nose of the aircraft. (SMAM.)

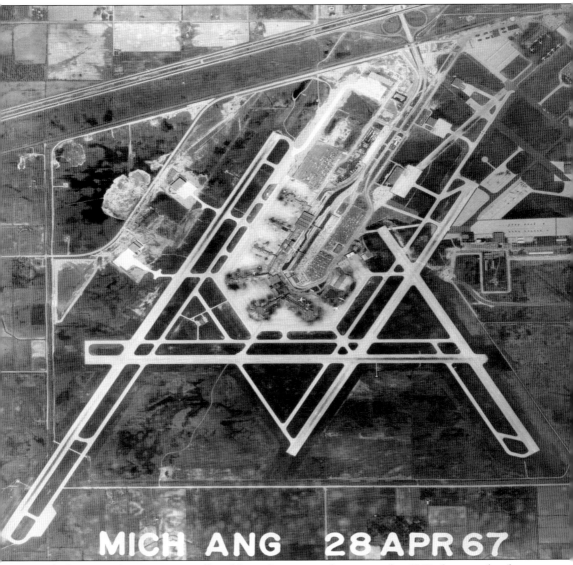

With the original runways are still visible in the upper-right corner, this 1967 photograph taken by the Air National Guard shows how much the airport had expanded since its inception. The guard occupied the east side of the airport until December 1971. With federal cutbacks and the growth of commercial air traffic, it was not practical for Detroit-Wayne Major to have a military establishment with high security. There was also a Nike missile base, established in the 1950s, to protect the airport and the region's industrial facilities, located just south of the Air National Guard facilities. (WCAA.)

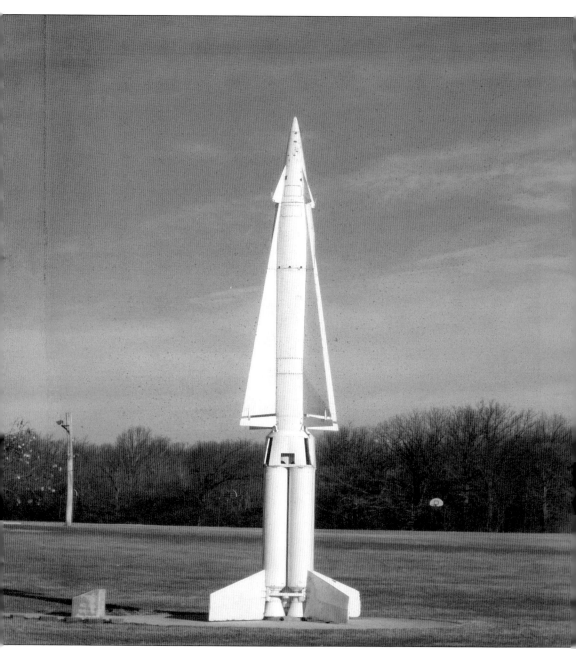

This was one type of missile at the base on standby 24 hours a day in case of an attack on the United States. Known as the Nike Hercules, this particular missile is unarmed but would have carried a nuclear payload; it stands where Nike base D-54 once operated in Riverview, Michigan, as a reminder of what Americans went through during the Cold War. The other missile stored at the Romulus base, the Ajax, had a single engine but did not carry a nuclear payload. (Author's collection.)

Five

SAFETY AND SECURITY

Since the opening of Wayne County Airport in 1930, there have always been unavoidable accidents. A handbook of safety procedures and rules was developed to help prevent accidents from occurring and to inform airport employees about what to do in case of emergencies. Today, security is crucial cog in airport operations. Employees, contractors, vendors, airline personnel, and government workers must have identification badges and abide by many rules.

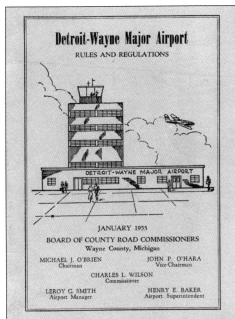

In the 1950s, it was important that ground personnel were trained in the use of the fire equipment since there were no permanent firemen at the airport. Wayne County relied on airport employees and the Air National Guard to take care of any situations that arose. (SMAM.)

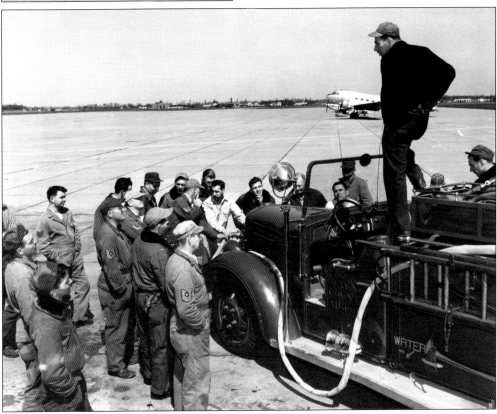

If the accident was civilian, the county was in charge and the guard provided support; the roles reversed if the accident was military. Here, Donald Hanchett from airport maintenance talks with guard personnel. (WHS.)

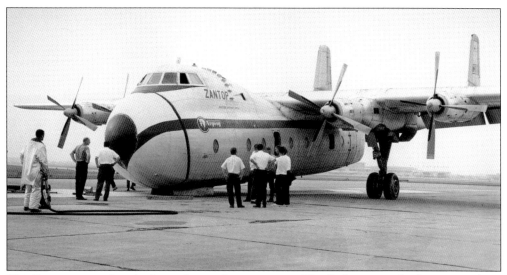

This Zantop cargo plane had a mishap with its nose gear. The flight crew and others are working to figure out what went wrong and assess the damage. Another worker, dressed in protective gear in case of a fire, waits with a hose. Minor accidents occur all the time, and all of them are taken seriously. (WCAA.)

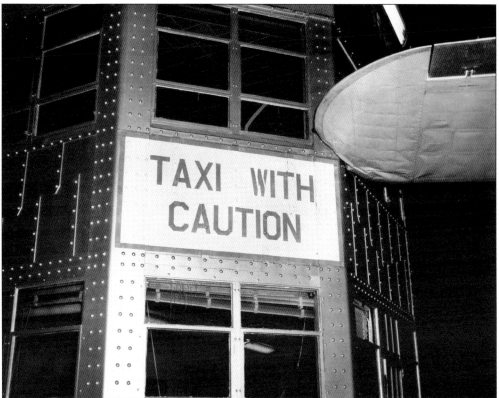

Many types of accidents can occur, especially when pilots fail to observe signs like this one outside the Air National Guard hangar. A pilot evidently thought he had enough clearance but hit the side of the building. (SMAM.)

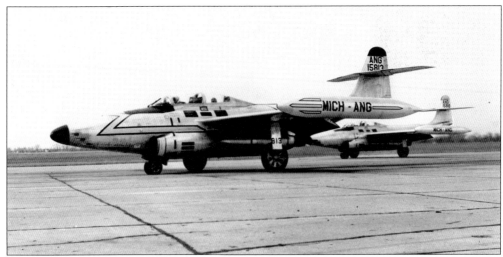

The F-89 Scorpion was an active aircraft in the Air National Guard. Unfortunately, there were structural flaws early on with this model—stress on the wings could cause them to rip off during hard maneuvers or at high speeds. In one instance in 1952, a wing ripped off during an air show at Detroit-Wayne Major. Pilot Maj. Donald Adams and radar operator Capt. Ed Kelly were killed, and five spectators were injured. (SMAM.)

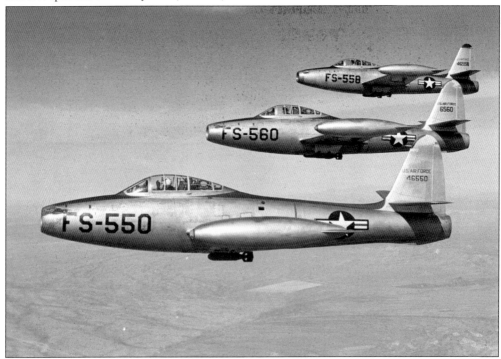

This photograph shows an F-84 Thunderjet, the type of plane T/Sgt. Robert A. Lewis was almost killed by when the jet intake nearly sucked him in while performing maintenance. S/Sgt. Joseph Cusenza noticed Lewis's legs hanging out the intake and immediately grabbed hold of them. M/Sgt. William Vilrody, in the cockpit testing the engine, did not know what was going on and noticed the engine sounding rough. Vilrody shut down the engine and was surprised to find Lewis mere inches from being shredded by the razor-sharp turbine blades. (SMAM.)

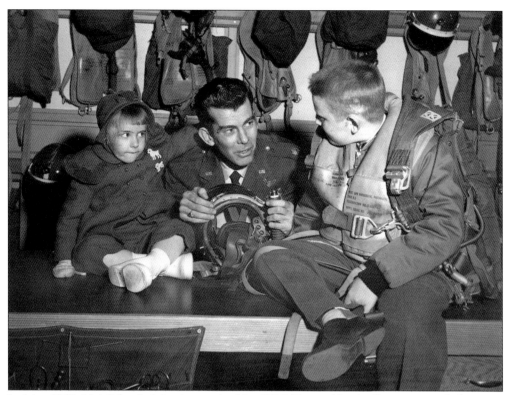

In May 1959, Maj. John L. Moutier crashed his RF-84F near Northville into a yard close to a group of five children. Two of the kids, three-year-old Elizabeth King and her 10-year-old brother David, spent several months in the hospital. They were seriously burned by blazing jet fuel when the plane crashed a mere 100 feet from them; the three others were unharmed. Moutier, from Belleville, parachuted to safety after his aircraft locked up and went into an uncontrolled ascent. The major and other members of the Air National Guard hosted the children, parents Eugene King (who was chief of the Northville Police Department) and his wife, and the rest of the King family for a tour and dinner at Detroit Metro. The children were shown how it was actually safe to fly, and David expressed an interest in joining the Air Force when he grew up. (SMAM.)

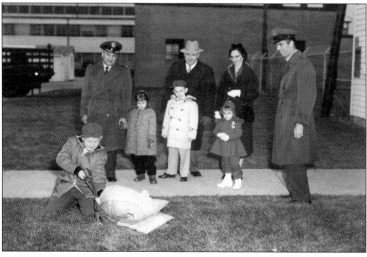

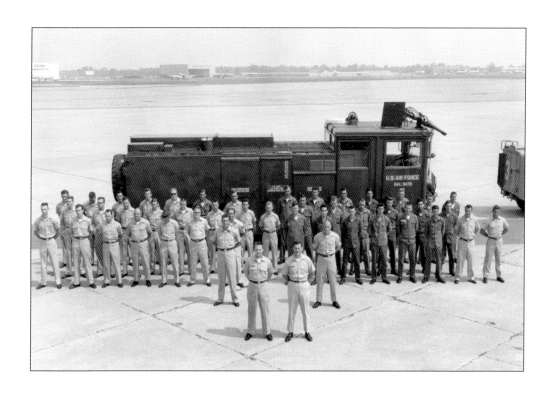

Above, members of the 191st Civil Engineers stand in front of their fire equipment. The truck could spray either a chemical foam or water to put out a fire. The training photograph below shows how a gun-type nozzle can be aimed at the fire without risking exposure to the flames; even though firemen wear flame-retardant suits, direct exposure is a high risk. The plane they were practicing on is an F-84 Thunderjet that was scrapped because of a faulty oxygen tank. (SMAM.)

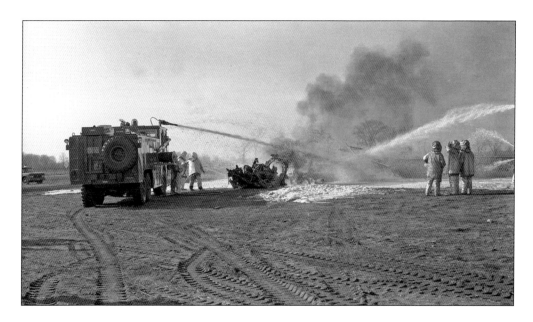

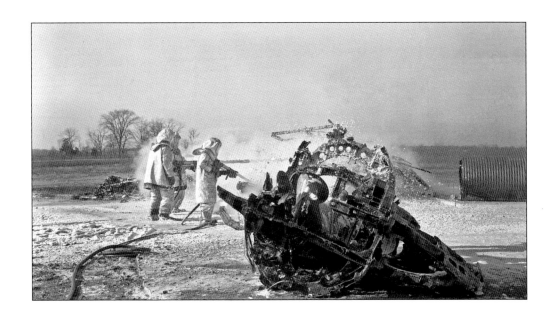

As told to the author and documented on these pages, Jim Koglin, a former Air National Guardsman, recalled the time spent practicing putting out fires. The trainers set a first test fire, and the blaze was immediately put out. They repeated the drill, and a second test fire was put out, again, without a problem. A third fire was set, but this time it had to burn itself out because they found the tanks in the fire truck were empty from the first two tests. (SMAM.)

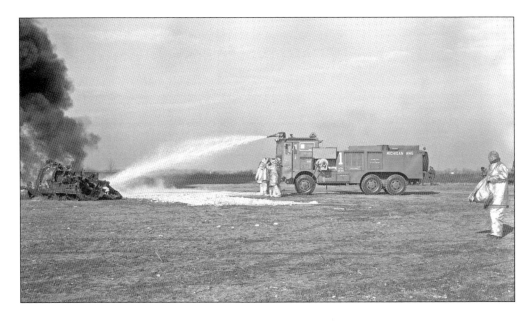

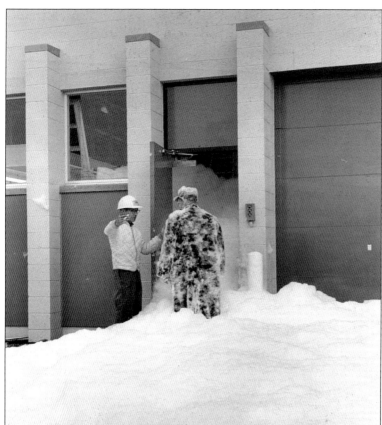

Fire prevention does not stop at aircraft; buildings must be protected as well. The two men in this photograph were testing out a flame-retardant foam system inside the hangar before the building was made available for the storage and maintenance of aircraft. (WCAA.)

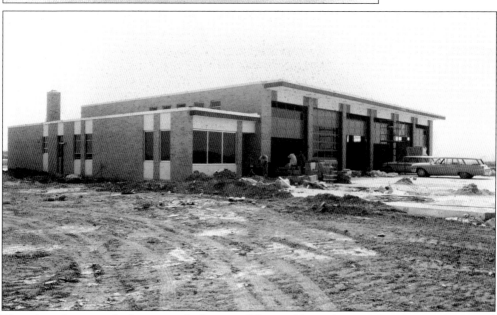

There have been two firehouses in the history of Detroit Metro Airport. Seen here is the second of the two, built in the mid-1960s, which was needed to store new and larger fire equipment. It is now the oldest firehouse at the airport, as the previous one was torn down. (WCAA.)

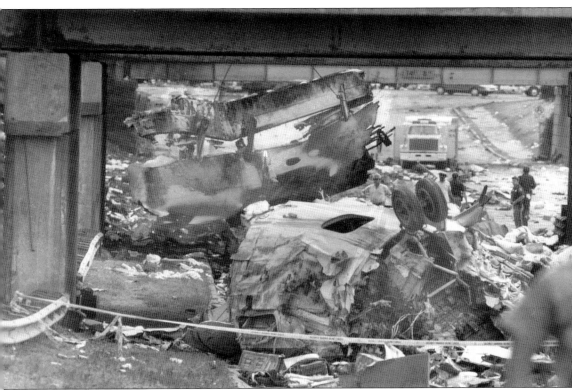

August 16, 1987, was a dark day for Detroit Metro Airport—Northwest Airlines Flight 255 crashed just after takeoff because the flight crew failed to go through the taxi checklist, and thus the flaps and slats were extended during takeoff. The plane was piloted by Capt. John R. Maus and copiloted by First Officer David J. Dodds. At a speed of 195 miles per hour, the plane first struck a light pole near the end of the runway before it ripped through the roof of a Avis car rental building and crashed into some cars just north of the Wick Road intersection. Breaking apart, the plane burst into flames and hit a railroad overpass and the Interstate 94 eastbound overpass. There were 156 fatalities, including 2 on the ground; those two fatalities were motorists, and five other people on the ground were injured, one seriously. One of the 148 passengers who died was Nick Vanos, a center for the Phoenix Suns basketball team. The only survivor was four-year-old Cecelia Cichan. (DN.)

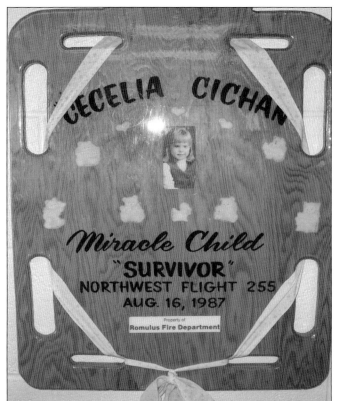

The lone survivor, Cecelia Cichan, was fastened to her seat. At the crash scene, she was overheard by volunteer fireman Dan Kish, who, with the aid of John Thiebe, removed wreckage to find her. Paramedic Roy Brindamour also assisted in rescuing Cichan from the rubble, and this backboard was used to carry her to the hospital. It now hangs at the Romulus Fire Department headquarters. (Author's collection.)

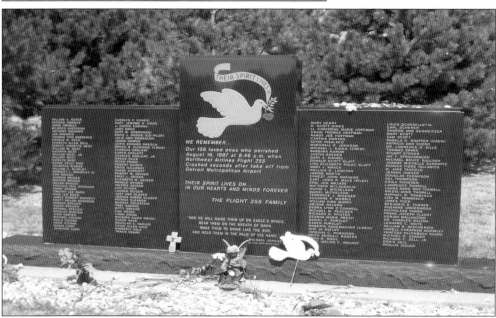

Family members of those who perished on Flight 255 raised money to build this memorial on the site where the plane met its end. It is located on a hill at Middlebelt Road and Interstate 94. There is no parking, and the memorial is only partly visible because of the pine trees planted around the area. (Author's collection.)

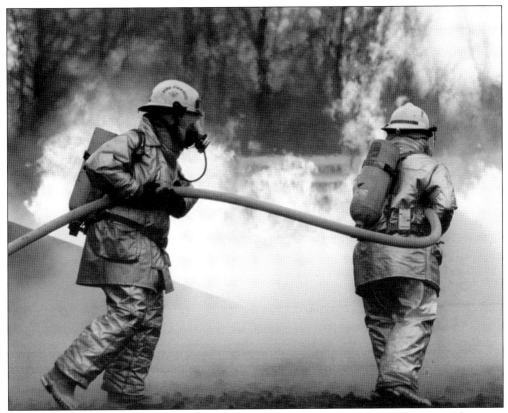

These firefighters are at the site known as the "burn pit," which is used for training in southeastern Michigan. The mock plane helps firefighters get the feel of working inside the close quarters of an airplane interior. (WCAA.)

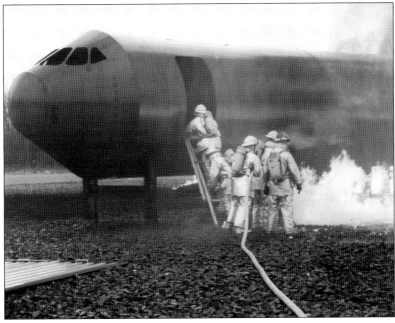

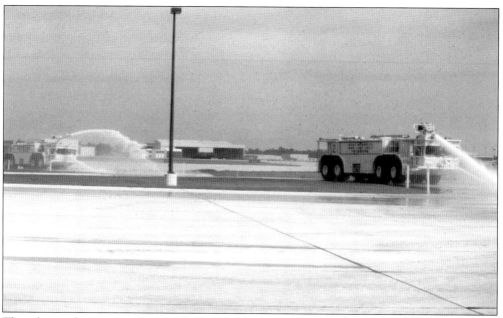

These heavy-duty fire trucks, the T1 1989 Oshkosh model, carry foam and water. They are very noticeable when the firefighters are out practicing. (RS.)

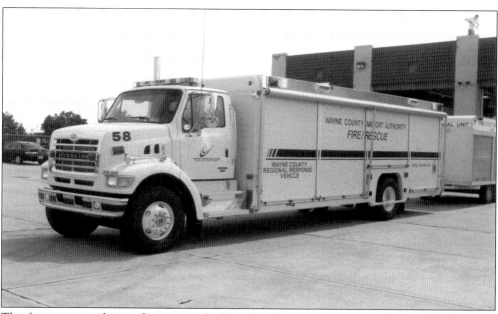

This fire rescue truck is used to treat multiple medical injuries in case of a plane crash. The truck is equipped with the necessary supplies to save lives and to handle casualties. (RS.)

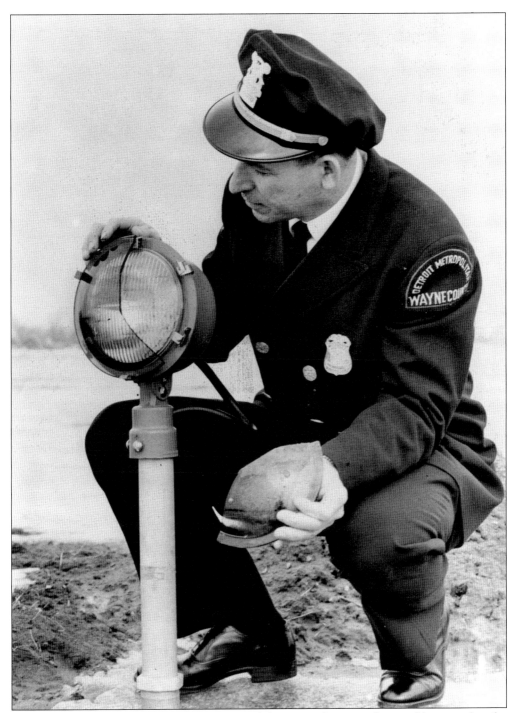

For many years, crime was not a concern around the airport because of its rural location, but the police were still occasionally called. Here, a Wayne County deputy checks out a broken airfield light lens that was shot out by a local hunter during apparent target practice. Crime started to pick up in the late 1950s, when the airport had become busier, and more people left their cars there. By 1965, the Wayne County Sheriff's Office began regular patrols through the airport. (WCAA.)

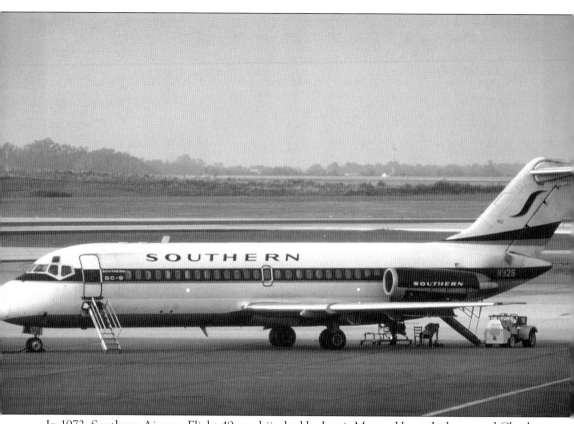

In 1972, Southern Airways Flight 49 was hijacked by Lewis Moore, Henry Jackson, and Charles Cale, who were all in trouble with the authorities at the time: Moore and Jackson in the Detroit area and Cale in Tennessee. The flight was hijacked in Birmingham, Alabama, and traveled to several locations in the United States (including Detroit Metro Airport), as well as Toronto, Canada, before landing in Chattanooga after threatening to crash the plane into a nuclear facility in Tennessee. Their ransom demands of $10 million were partially met with $2 million, and the plane then flew on to Havana. Once arriving in Cuba, the hijackers decided not to stay after negotiations failed. The plane headed back to the United States, where the pilot convinced the hijackers it needed fuel, so they stopped at McCoy Air Force Base in Orlando, Florida. At that point, they demanded to speak to President Nixon, which was not met, so they ordered the pilot to takeoff again. As it was about to liftoff, the FBI tried to end the ordeal by shooting out the tires, and the panicked hijackers shot and injured the copilot en route back to Cuba. Once setting down on a foam-covered runway on the island, authorities promptly captured the fugitives and confiscated the money as passengers were released. Later, the FBI was criticized for how it handled the situation. (Photograph by R.A. Schofield.)

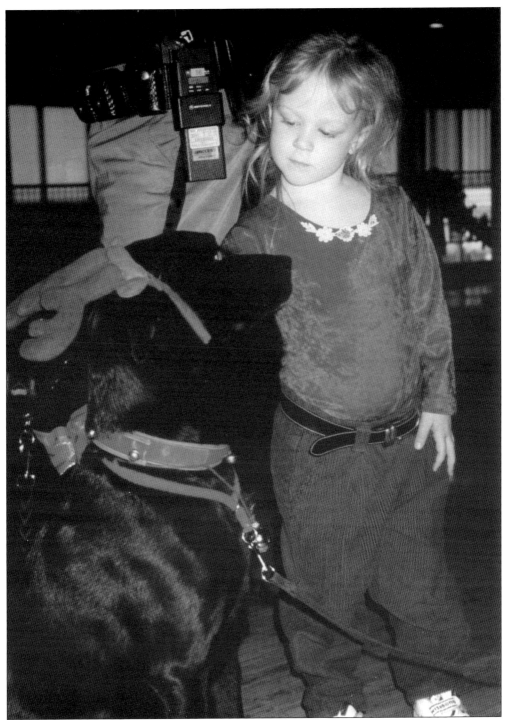

In 1985, Deputy Sheriff Bruce Preston and his K-9 partner Angel were assigned to the airport to check for explosives in baggage. Angel, one of two dogs working with security, also provided good public relations. A young lady pets Angel, who is wearing antlers for the occasion, in this 1985 holiday photograph. (WCAA.)

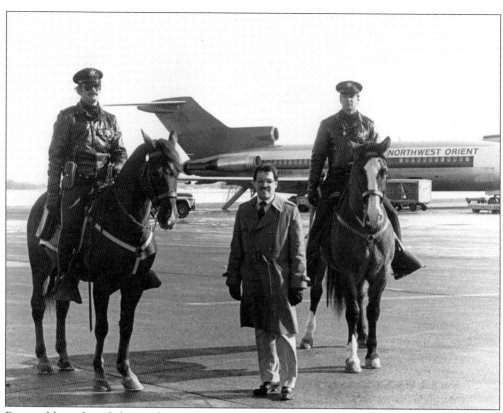

Pictured here from left to right are Dan Michaelson on his horse Shamrock, Wayne County sheriff Robert Ficano, and Paul Nowak on his horse Nicholas. Deputies from the Wayne County Sheriff's Office Mounted Unit began working at the airport because much of the surrounding land was wooded and difficult for vehicles to access. With no facility there to accommodate them, the horses were brought to the airport in a trailer every day. (PN.)

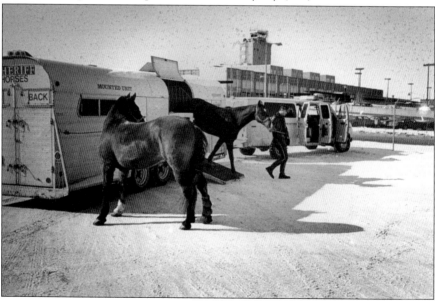

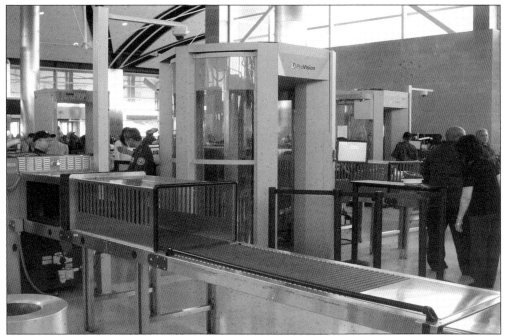

This machine, known as the AIT (Advanced Imagery Technology), is the latest technology utilized by the Transportation Security Administration (TSA) to check people for contraband. A person walks in with hands above his or her head, is scanned, and the machine indicates whether something is suspicious on that person. If something out of the ordinary is detected, the individual is pulled aside and checked for that abnormality. (Author's collection.)

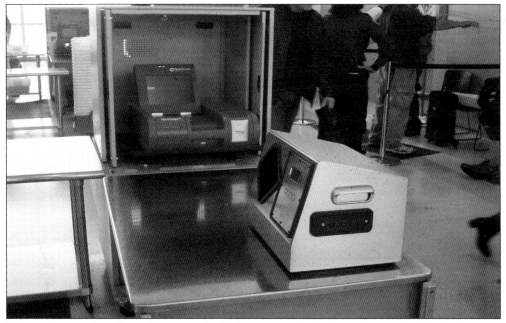

The machine in the cabinet, known as a ETD (Electronic Trace Detector), is used to check electronic devices like laptops and DVD players for explosives. The machine in the foreground, a liquid tester, is used to check fluids like baby formula or medical liquids for explosives. (Author's collection.)

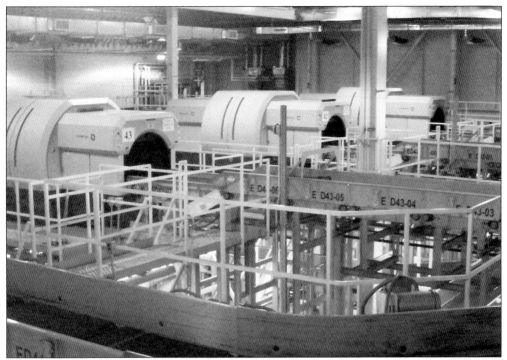

Every piece of baggage and every package checked in at the service desk will be processed through a CT scanner machine. If there are no abnormal objects inside the baggage, it goes directly to the loading area for the passenger's scheduled flight. If something seems suspicious, a TSA official will physically check the baggage, place a note inside the package, and seal it with tape to alert the passenger that it has been checked. (Author's collection.)

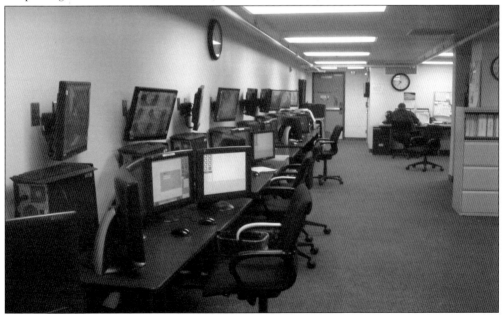

Every X-ray machine has a monitor, and a master room contains the monitors in a place where they can be viewed away from the public eye. (Author's collection.)

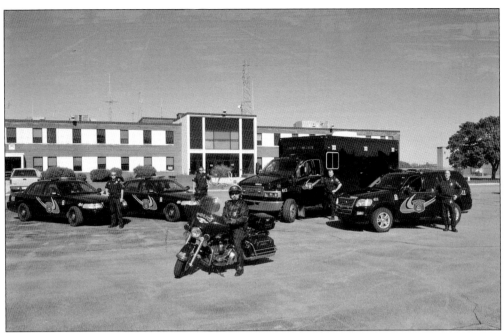

Today, the airport has its own police department that operates independent from the county. The airport police headquarters is in the old Air National Guard building. Even though this department works for the airport, it also provides support for local police departments. Although horses are no longer needed to get around the airport, it still utilizes various modes of transportation. (Above, VP; below, Author's collection.)

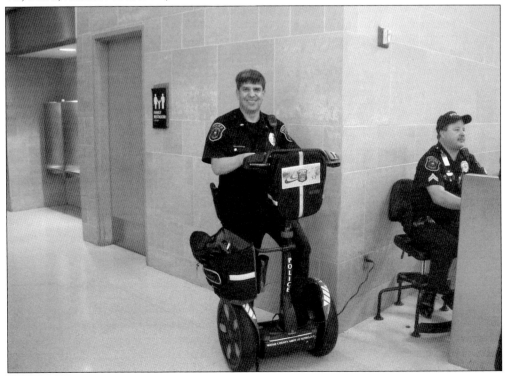

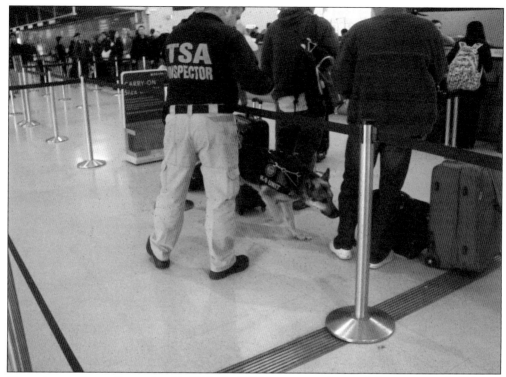

Since the attacks on September 11, 2001, the TSA has retained several dogs as part of a K-9 unit to help detect explosives; most of them work in and around the air-cargo facilities. Normally, the dogs do not check passenger bags, but these photographs demonstrate how trainers Brian J. Clinton (above, with Rex the German shepherd) and Amanda Mostek (below, with Bubba the golden retriever) check luggage for possible explosives. (Author's collection.)

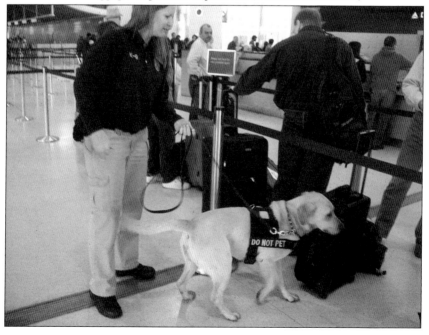

Six

Detroit Metropolitan Airport

In 1955, the US government wanted to move civilian airlines and air-cargo companies from Willow Run Airport to Detroit-Wayne Major Airport. By 1957, expansion of the airport was okayed with a $10.6 million grant provided by the Civil Aeronautics Administration and the Michigan Department of Aeronautics. A new terminal was constructed, with a hotel, restaurant, and a 10,500-foot-long runway, and the airport was renamed Detroit Metropolitan Wayne County Airport. The new terminal opened in 1958 and was named after Leroy C. Smith, chairman of the Wayne County Road Commission. American Airlines, Northwest Orient, Allegheny, Pan Am, and British Overseas moved operations from Willow Run Airport, and Detroit Metro Airport became the first inland airport in the United States to be brought into the jet age. The Federal Aviation Administration foresaw that Detroit Metro was still growing and recommended further construction to accommodate the ever-increasing number of people travelling by airplane.

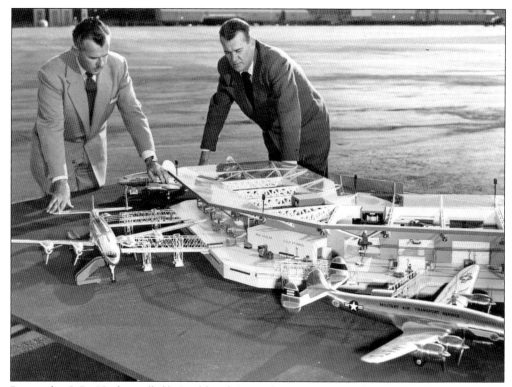

Pictured is L.R. Hackney (left), Lockheed Aircraft Corporation sales engineer and air-freight specialist, with Gordon Stanton, manager of airport development from Lockheed Air Terminal Inc. They are looking over a model of a proposed cargo terminal that would be fully automated, with conveyor belts that mate with aircraft to off-load and shuttle the freight to and from the terminal. (WCDPS.)

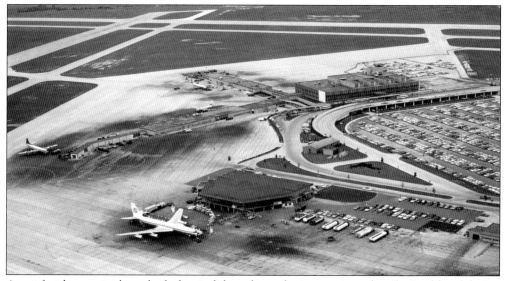

An airfreight terminal was built, but it did not have the innovations that the Lockheed design offered. It remained there until a newer warehouse for American Airline Cargo came in as a replacement. (WCAA.)

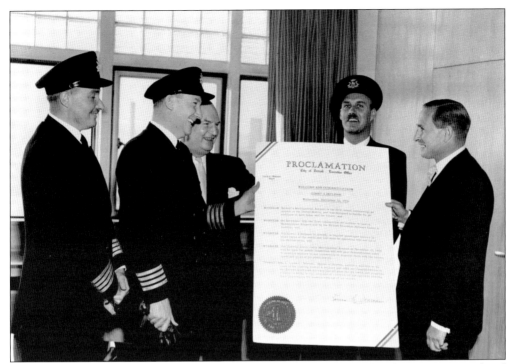

The first passenger jet to land at Detroit Metro Airport was a de Havilland Comet 4, owned and operated by British Overseas Airways Corporation (BOAC), that flew in on November 12, 1958. Mayor Louis C. Miriani had a proclamation stated that British Overseas Airlines was the first to make an inland landing in the United States with a passenger jetliner. Pilot Thomas Stoney is holding the proclamation with directing manager of BOAC Basyl Stonepiece (center) and assistant airport manager James Davey (far right). Below, the de Havilland Comet 4 is captured in flight. (Above, WCAA; below, BAHC.)

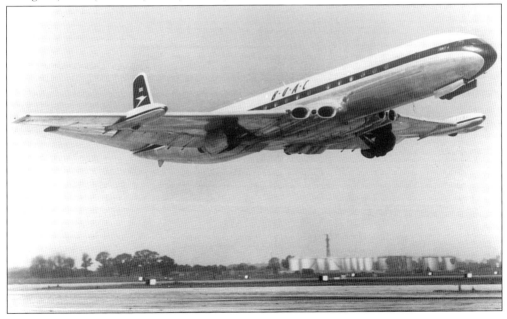

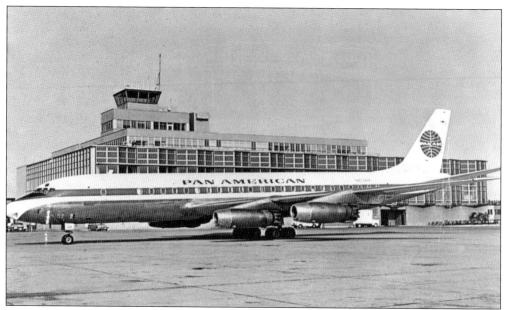

Pan American World Airways, which flew mostly Douglas DC-8s, was British Overseas Airways Corporation's competitor for passengers looking for overseas flights out of Detroit Metro. Pan Am was the largest international air carrier in the United States during the late 1950s. (WCAA.)

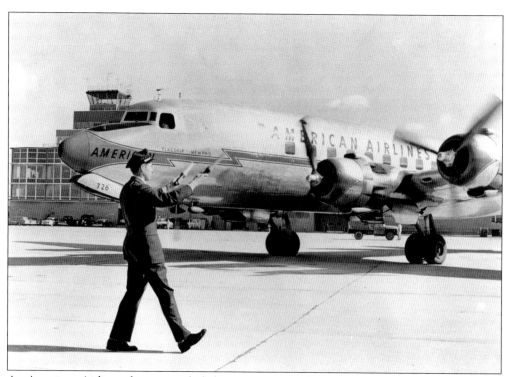

An American Airlines plane is marshaled into position on the apron mat for arrival and deplaning of cargo and passengers. American, which relocated from Willow Run Airport, signed a 30-year contract in 1956 to move its base operations to Detroit Metro. (WCAA.)

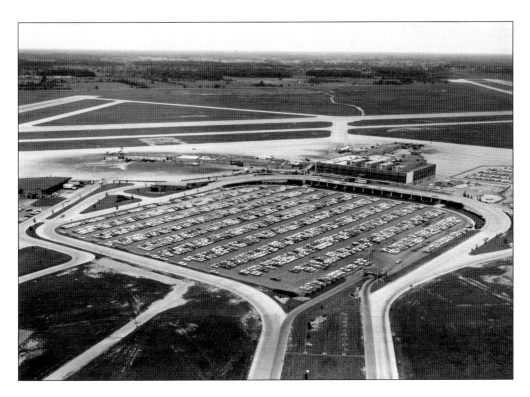

Building a two-level road for airport access simplified the flow of traffic, as designers placed departures on the top level and arrivals on the bottom level. Another important addition was a free shuttle bus from the spacious parking lot to the airport terminal. (WCAA.)

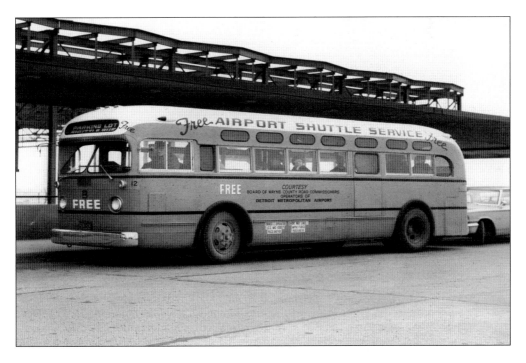

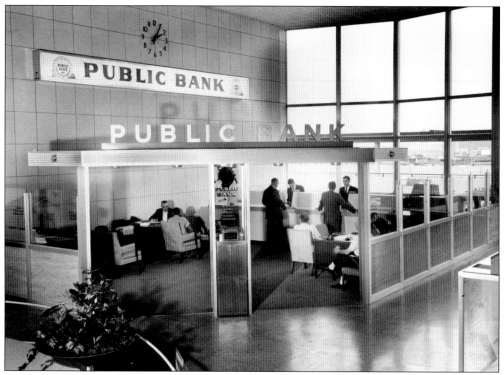

By 1960, Public Bank opened a branch office for travelers who wanted easy access to cash and international travelers who needed to exchange currency. (WCAA.)

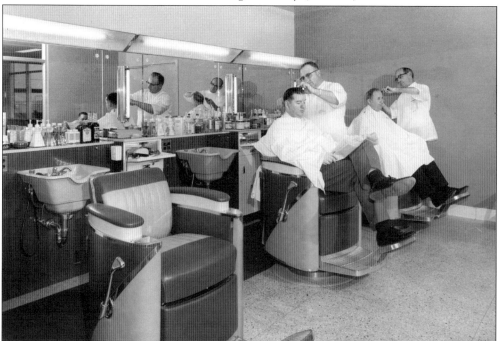

A barbershop was another convenience in the terminal, offering a place where business travelers could spruce up for important meetings in Detroit or out of town. (WCAA.)

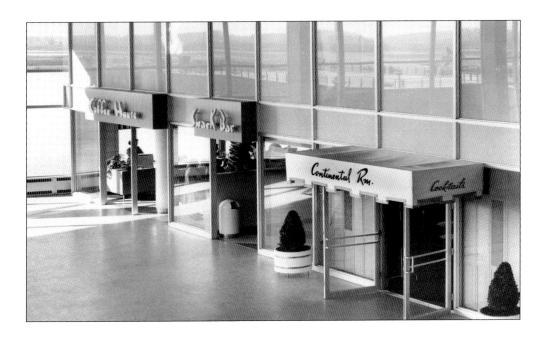

There were a variety of places to eat in the Smith terminal, from a basic sandwich shop to fine dining. The Coffee House (below) offered travelers a nice view of the airport, and the Continental Room provided fine dining to the traveler who could afford it. (WCAA.)

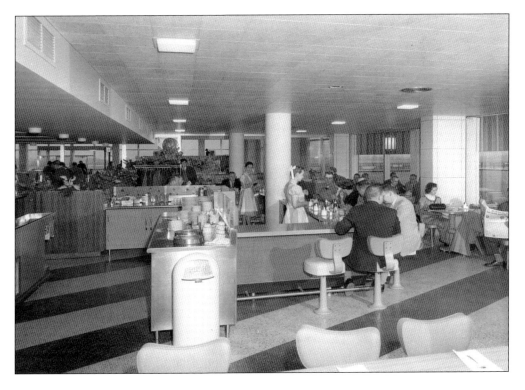

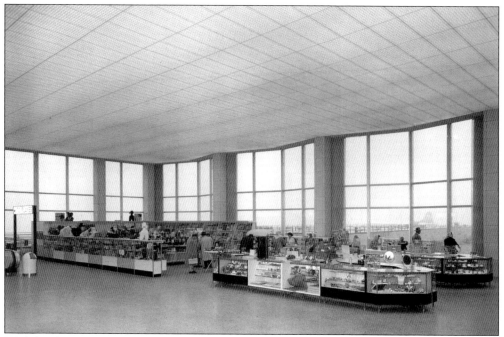

With banking, dining, and a barbershop, the airport had become a small city. There was also a shop that sold magazines, snacks, souvenirs, and replacements for items travelers may have accidentally forgotten. There was even a motel for passengers who needed to stay overnight at the airport. (WCAA.)

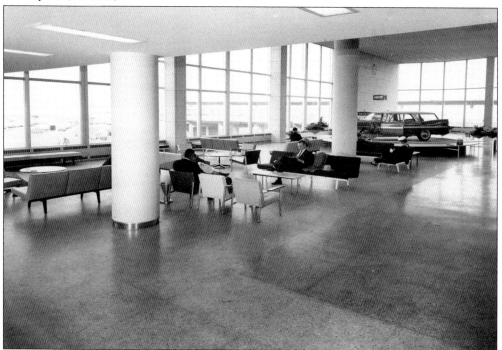

The waiting areas offered ample seating for weary travelers and often had cars on display from local dealerships. (WCAA.)

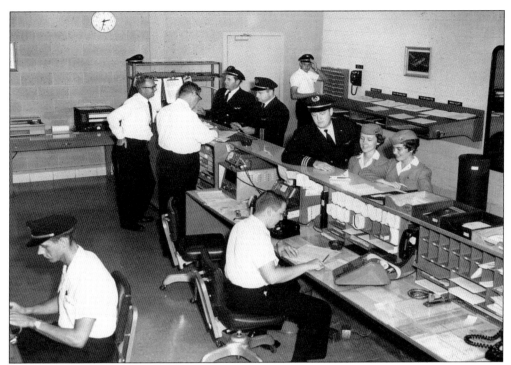

When the Smith Terminal was first built, there were two check-in rooms for flight crews on the north and south sides; what terminal a person went to was dictated by the airline he or she worked for. Crews consisted of pilots, copilots, engineers, and stewardesses (now known as flight attendants). (WCAA.)

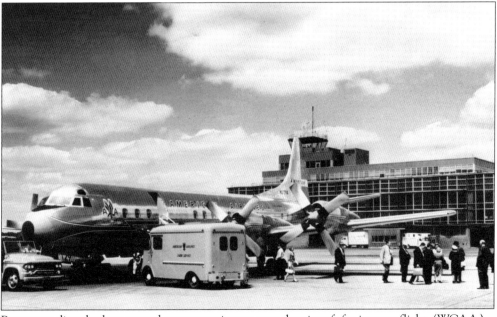

Passengers disembark as ground support arrives to prep the aircraft for its next flight. (WCAA.)

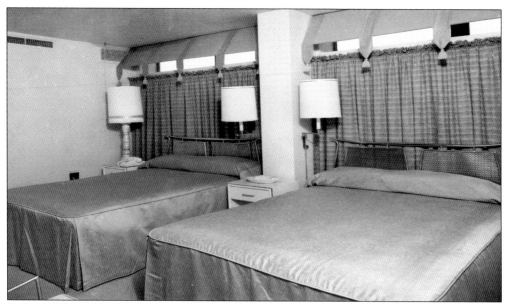

Before a full-sized hotel was built at the airport, the L.C. Smith Terminal had a hotel on the top floor. It had several rooms and a conference center that doubled as a banquet hall. (WCAA.)

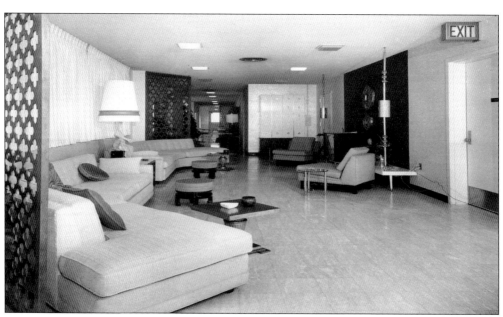

The hotel hallway was wide enough for furnishings that allowed overnight passengers a place to relax and socialize. (WCAA.)

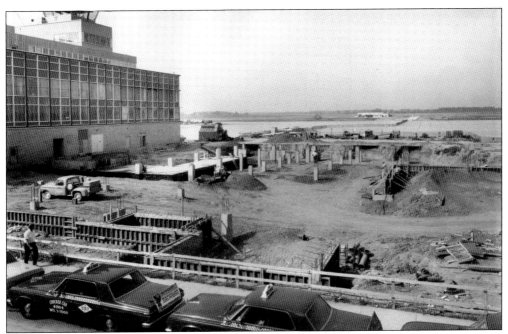

In 1959, the FAA proposed construction to expand Detroit Metro Airport to accommodate the projected increase of over five million passengers over the next six years and offered to fund it. The original observation deck on the Smith Terminal was removed and replaced with a new one at the north end of the terminal. (WCAA.)

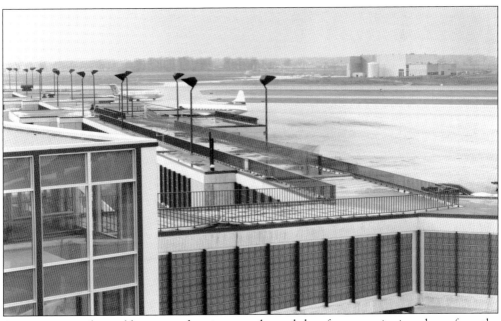

Sometimes, people would come to the airport and spend the afternoon viewing planes from the observation deck. Coin-operated magnifying viewers could be used to get a closer look. (WCAA.)

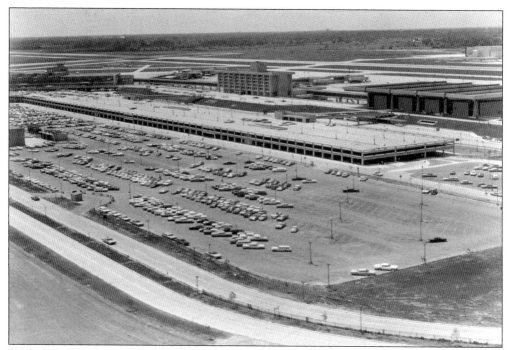

With the increase of flights, the airport became busier during the late 1960s. A parking structure with walkways that connected to the different departure levels was erected to accommodate the anticipated overflow of travelers. (WCAA.)

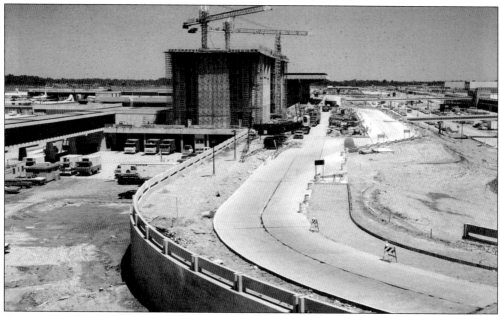

Having a hotel at the airport would bring in revenue, and with the increase of passengers a new hotel was constructed in 1967. The hotel rooms in the Smith Terminal were converted to office space. (WCAA.)

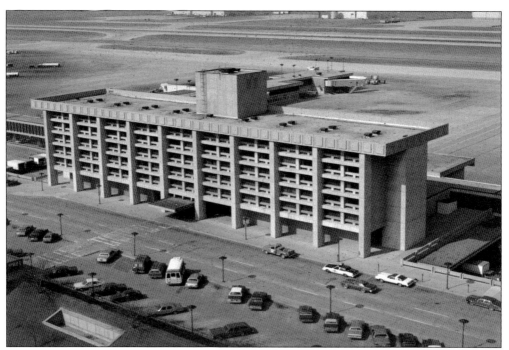

The hotel was situated between the Smith and Davey Terminals and offered easy access to whatever airline hotel guests had flight reservations for. A causeway that went through the hotel linked the Smith and Davey Terminals. (WCAA.)

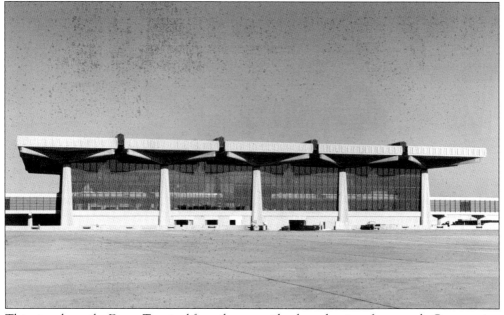

This view shows the Davey Terminal from the ramp side where the aircraft approach. Construction on this terminal started in the mid-1960s, when the number of flights going in and out of the airport was rapidly increasing. The Davey Terminal was named after airport manager James Davey, who was there for its dedication in 1974. (WCAA.)

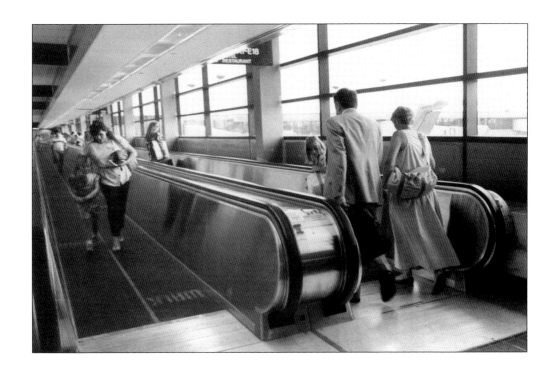

Inside the causeway that joined the terminals was a conveyor-belt walkway to allow passengers a convenient way to ride or walk to their flight gate more quickly. (WCAA.)

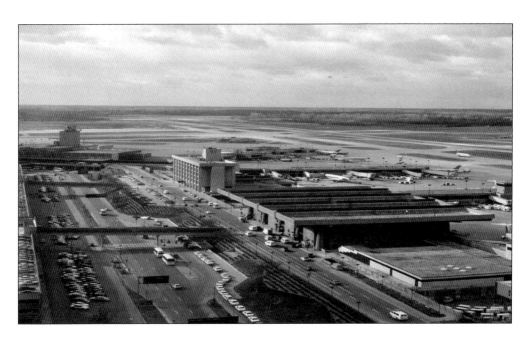

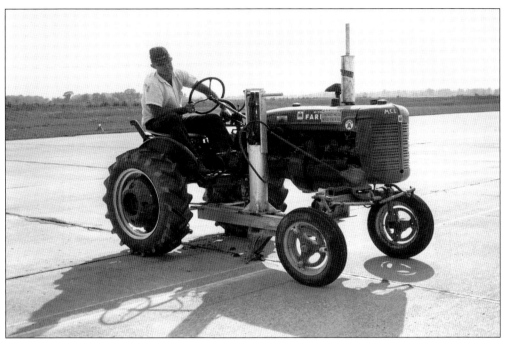

In the early 1960s, much of the concrete around the older buildings and runways needed resurfacing, including the Air National Guard apron. An outside contractor was hired to do the job, which included replacing tar between the concrete sections (shown here). (WCAA.)

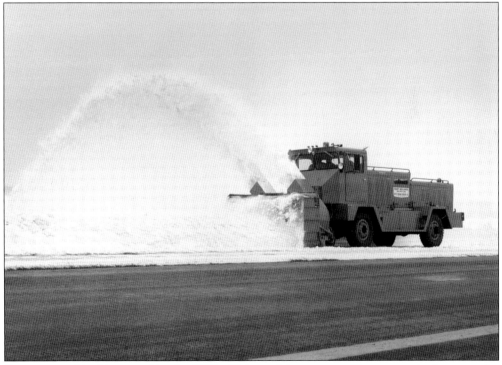

Snow removal had improved by the 1960s. This machine operates like an oversized present-day snowblower, throwing the snow in any direction the operator chooses. (WCDPS.)

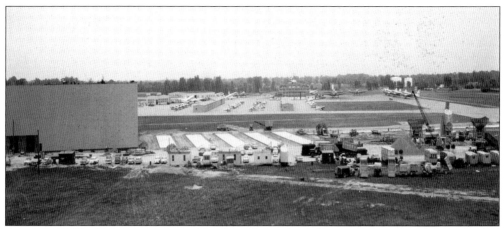

After World War II, big corporations like Great Lakes Steel, Rockwell Spring and Axle, the AC Spark Plug Division of General Motors, and Ford Motor Company, among others, kept private planes at the airport. (WCAA.)

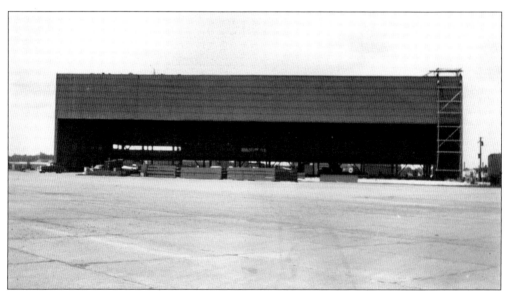

In the early 1960s, Ford Motor Company had a new hangar built at Detroit Metro to store company aircraft. Ford had kept the company aircraft at the airport since the 1930s and believed it needed a modern facility. In 2009, the company went through restructuring and closed its hangar at Detroit Metro. General Motors also closed its hangar after bankruptcy and criticism from the US Congress for flying private instead of commercial when traveling to Washington, DC, in 2008 to ask for a loan. (WCAA.)

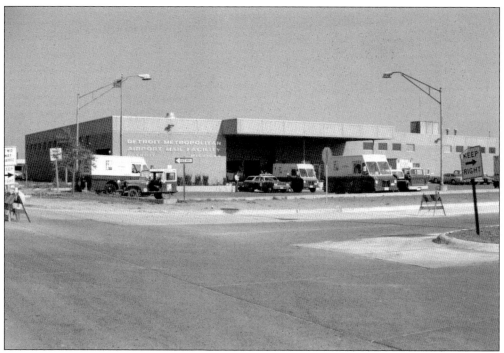

One of the reasons the airport came into existence was the mail service, so the US Postal Service had a post office and sorting facility built at the airport in 1967 for quicker processing. It was a 24-hour operation at this facility, with several hundred employees working in three shifts. (WCAA.)

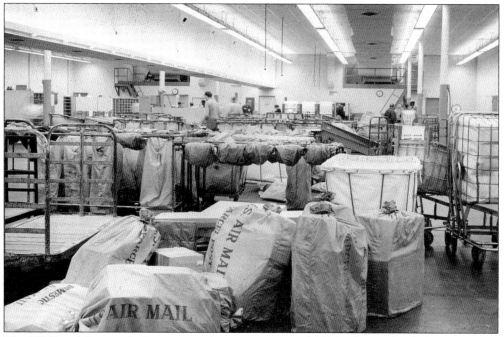

The US Postal Service facility remained in operation until 2008, when it decided to contract a company using a different facility to sort the mail. (WCAA.)

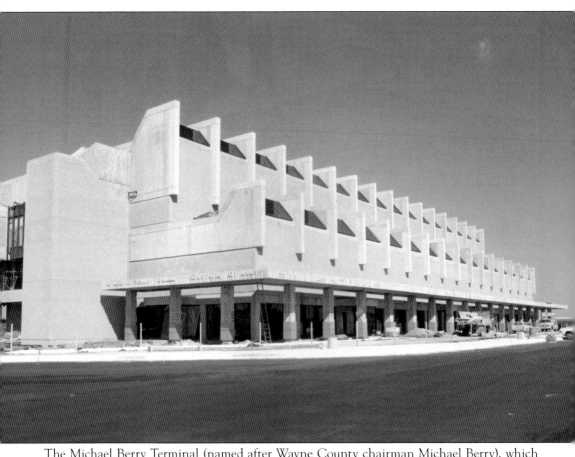

The Michael Berry Terminal (named after Wayne County chairman Michael Berry), which opened in 1974, became the international terminal at Detroit Metro. US Customs processed passengers from other countries by checking their credentials and inspecting their baggage. The terminal contained private clubs for first-class and business passengers of British Airways, KLM, and Lufthansa. Northwest/KLM moved to the McNamara Terminal in 2002; British Airways, Lufthansa, and Reliant Airlines followed, leaving only Spirit, USA 3000, and charter airlines until the closing of the Berry Terminal. British Airways eventually left the airport in 2008 when London's Heathrow Airport was opened to other carriers, including Northwest. (WCAA.)

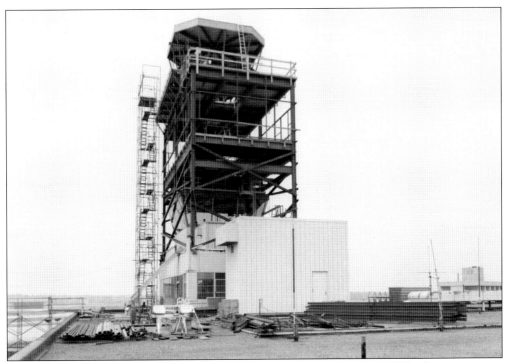

The growth of the airport and the addition of longer runways made it difficult to see across the field. Instead of building a new tower, the old tower was raised as it was being used. It was completed in 1973. (WCAA.)

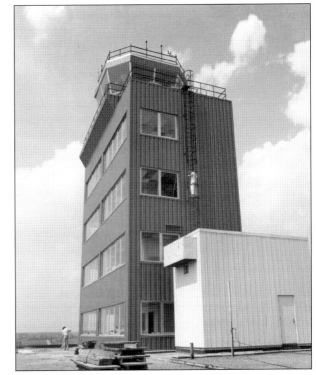

When the tower was under construction, there was an electrical fire in the new section above the old tower. It had to be evacuated, causing a short shutdown of air traffic into and out of the airport. Now, all that remains of the old tower are the interior cinder blocks and the stairwell. (WCAA.)

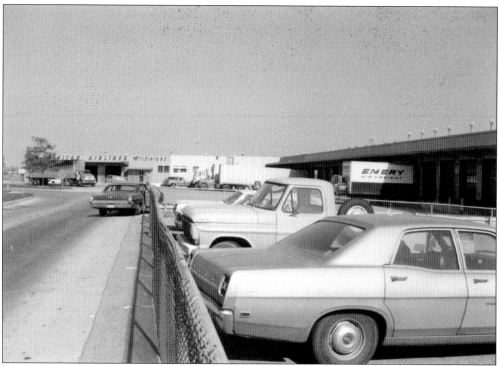

When airplanes started to become larger and had more room available in the bellies of the aircraft, airlines such as American started shipping cargo on passenger flights. This enabled the airlines to save on fuel and avoid unnecessary cargo flights, and it also enhanced revenue from these passenger flights. (WCAA.)

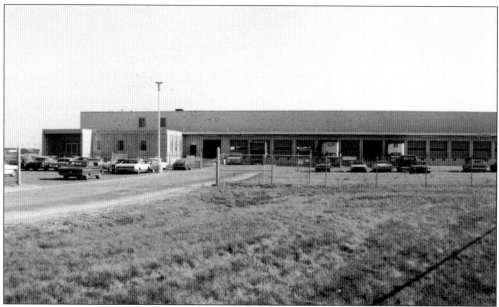

By 1970, Flying Tiger—one of the top air-cargo companies in the United States—had a new facility on the west side of the airport, where it serviced its aircraft and contracted out to load and unload for other air cargo companies. (WCAA.)

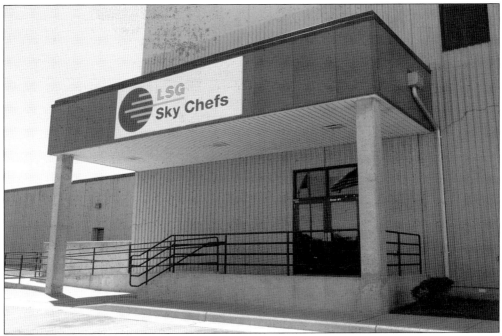

LSG Sky Chefs, located on airport property, was founded in 1974 and currently services six airlines at Detroit Metro Airport, providing over 25,000 meals on 350 flights per day. (LSG.)

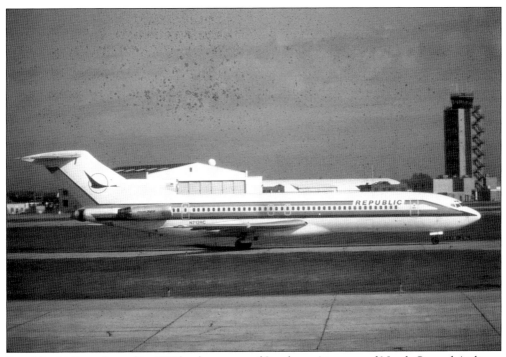

Republic Airlines, formed in 1979 by the merger of Southern Airways and North Central Airlines, had headquarters at Minneapolis–St. Paul International Airport; however, Detroit Metro Airport was Republic's major hub. Republic was purchased by Northwest in 1986. (TL.)

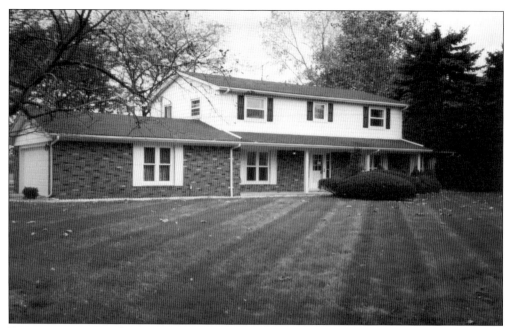

From 1996 to 2006, the FAA sponsored a program called Airport Improvement Funding. This funding allowed local residents in the flight path of airports to add sound insulation in their homes. A demonstration house was set up outside the Detroit Metro to educate people about how they could effectively insulate their homes. Five years after the program ended, this house was demolished in 2011. (WCAA.)

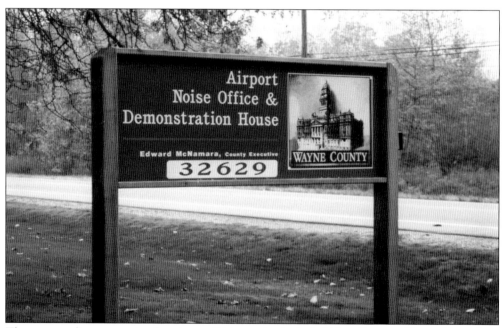

The surrounding towns in the airport flight paths included New Boston, Huron Township, Romulus, Taylor, Dearborn, and Westland. Any home built before 1990 was eligible for the program. (WCAA.)

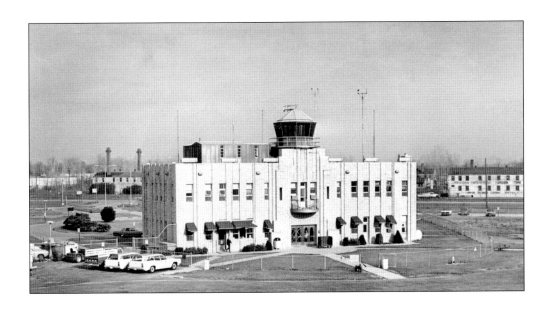

In 1973, Federal Express moved its Detroit-area operation from Willow Run Airport to Detroit Metro Airport and worked out of two offices in the old Executive Terminal. At first, only five employees worked there, managing the one inbound flight and one outbound flight per day. The plane used by Federal Express was a Dassault Falcon 20. On average, 30 packages were brought in each day, with employees responsible for delivery to the Greater Detroit Area and Toledo, Ohio. (Above, WCAA; below, FDX.)

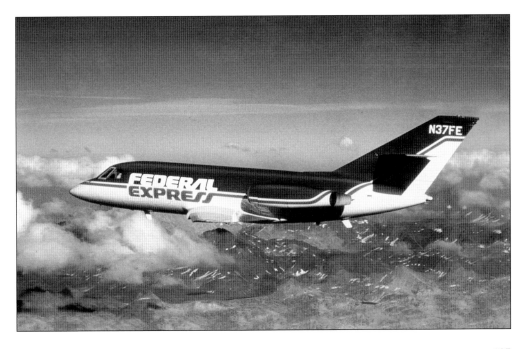

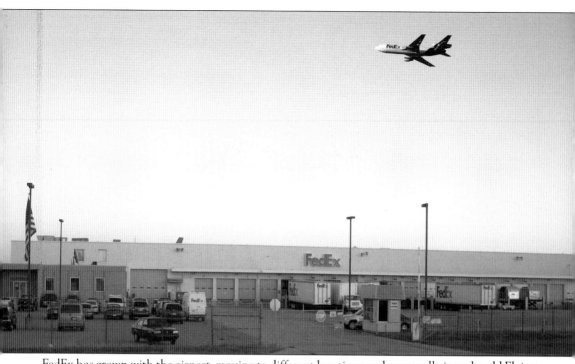

FedEx has grown with the airport, moving to different locations and eventually into the old Flying Tiger building (after FedEx purchased the company). FedEx gives back to the communities where it operates by participating in charity work. The company supports the United Way, March of Dimes, and the US military. (Author's collection.)

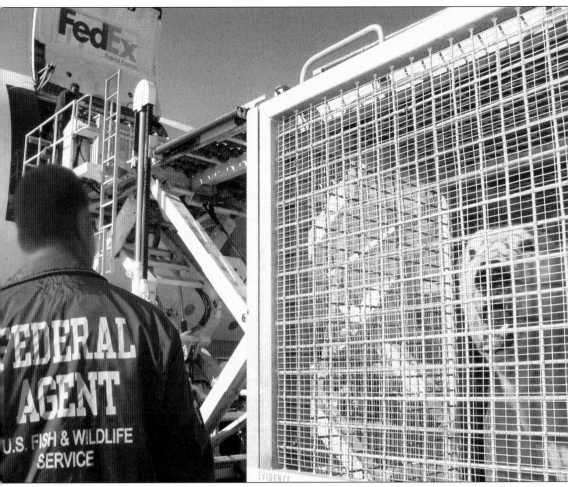

FedEx also transports animals in rescues or emergencies. In 2002, six polar bears were seized from the Circo Hermanos Suarez (Suarez Brothers Circus) in Puerto Rico. Several US zoos prepared to adopt the animals, and FedEx volunteered to fly them to their new homes. After being held in quarantine in customs, the bears were taken to the FedEx hub in Memphis, Tennessee, where they were transferred to flights that would transport them to the zoos. Peering out of the cage, one of the rescued polar bears appears to a bit curious about the camera. (FDX.)

United States Department of the Interior

FISH AND WILDLIFE SERVICE
Washington, D.C. 20240

IN REPLY REFER TO:
FWS/LE ADM 4-05

AUG 1 1 2003

Manager, Ramp Operations
FedEx Express

Romulus, Michigan 48242-0001

Dear Mr. Dirette:

Last November, FedEx Express, at company expense, transported six polar bears from San Juan, Puerto Rico, to the company's hub in Memphis, Tennessee, and then on to three mainland zoos scattered throughout the United States. The bears, which were in poor health, had been seized by U.S. Fish and Wildlife Service special agents for alleged violations that included failing to maintain the animals under humane and healthful conditions.

The successful completion of this complex animal rescue mission, which involved orchestrating flights, ensuring appropriate transport conditions, and arranging departures and/or arrivals at five different airports for animals weighing as much as 1,200 pounds each, would not have been possible without the assistance and expertise provided by you and your colleagues at FedEx Express.

I want to express my sincere thanks for your efforts on the ground, the contributions of other FedEx Express staff, and the company's generosity. The bears have thrived at their new homes, enjoying professional care and safe, species-appropriate living conditions.

We applaud the professionalism and "can do" spirit of the FedEx Express team that planned and carried out this complicated animal transport operation. Please know that your contributions and those of your company are much appreciated.

Thank you for helping us make a difference for wildlife!

Sincerely,

Steve Williams

DIRECTOR

The people involved in the careful planning of the bears' transportation worked with the US Department of Interior's Fish and Wildlife Service. This letter of thanks was presented to Matt Dirette, manager of ramp operations, for his involvement in the transport of the polar bears. (FDX.)

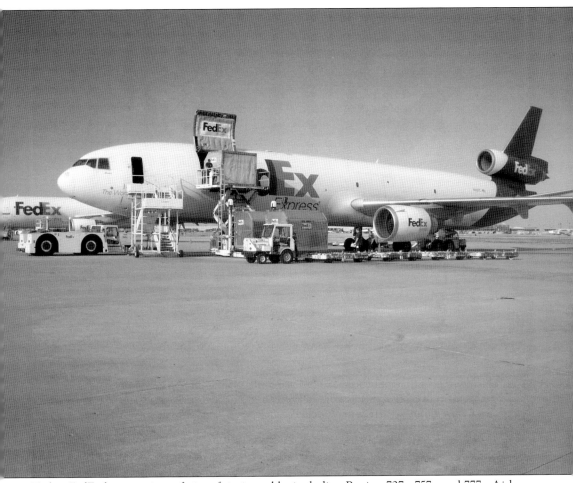

Today, FedEx has a variety of aircraft in its stable, including Boeing 727s, 757s, and 777s; Airbus A300s and A310s; and MD-10s and MD-11s. The Detroit ramp is not certified to accommodate the Boeing 757s and 777s. On average, the Detroit ramp services eight flights a day: one inbound and three outbound flights in the evening and three inbound and one outbound flight in the morning. Packages are sorted and trucked to stations in the Greater Detroit Area, Canada, and Toledo, Ohio. In the evening, packages are picked up from the stations and brought back to the airport to be sorted and flown out for distribution in the United States and around the world. (Author's collection.)

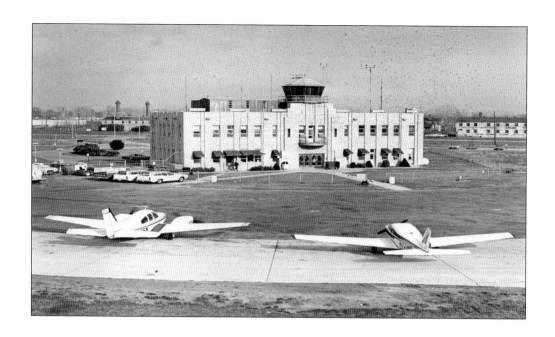

This is a late-1960s photograph of the old Executive Terminal. Today, the control-tower portion is gone because the building is in the flight path of a runway. There is a fence line between the aircraft and the building in the image above; according to a current employee, when The Beatles arrived in Detroit for a concert, fans knocked down the fence, and the airport never replaced it. Aircraft Service International Group currently occupies the Executive Terminal. (Above, WCAA; below, author's collection.)

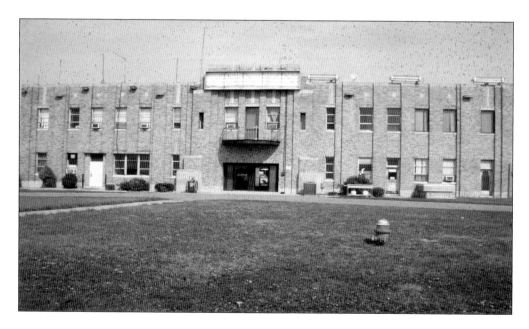

YES M!CH!GAN

Aviation

MICHIGAN AERONAUTICS COMMISSION · EST. 1929

OFFICIAL PUBLICATION, MICHIGAN AERONAUTICS COMMISSION, DEPARTMENT OF TRANSPORTATION

JAMES J. BLANCHARD, Governor

VOLUME 18   OCTOBER/NOVEMBER, 1985   NUMBER 7

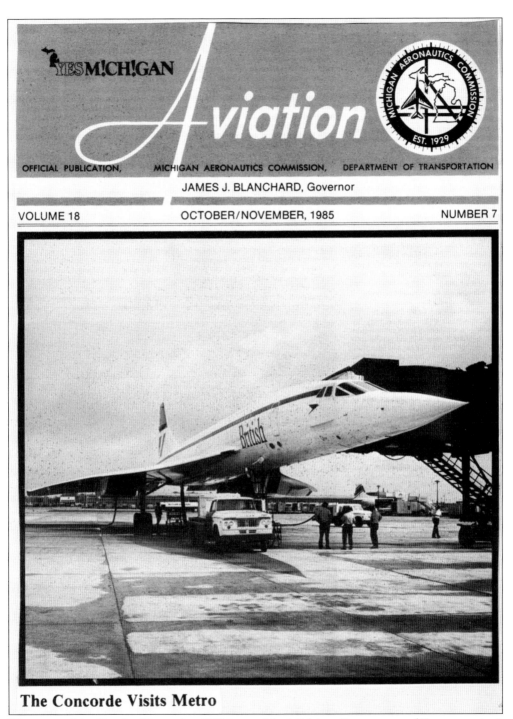

The Concorde Visits Metro

The cover of the October/November 1985 issue of the Michigan Department of Transportation's *Aviation* magazine shows the British Airways Concorde at one of the gates at Detroit Metro Airport. (MDOT.)

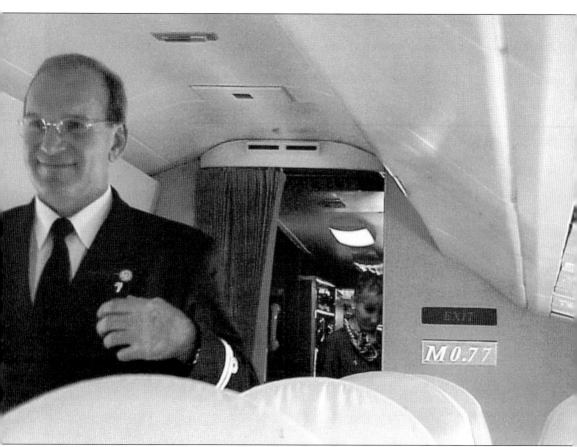

On August 23, 1985, British Airways landed not one, but two Concordes at Detroit Metro—at the same time. There were tens of thousands of spectators, causing traffic jams along Interstate 94. Nomads, a travel club that flew to different places around the world, chartered the flights to London, England. British Airways also landed the first commercial Boeing 777 at Detroit Metro. The last time the Concorde landed at the airport was in May 1999, when Nomads chartered a flight to Paris. The Concorde has since been retired, and Nomads filed for bankruptcy in 2011. (WCAA.)

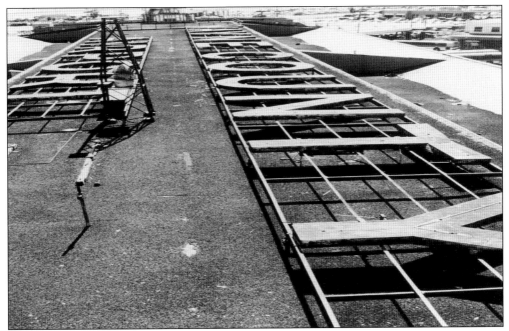

This is the last known photograph of the roof of Hangar 278 before it began to deteriorate. At the time, the structure was leased to the Hertz car rental company. Today, no one is allowed inside because of unsafe conditions. (WCAA.)

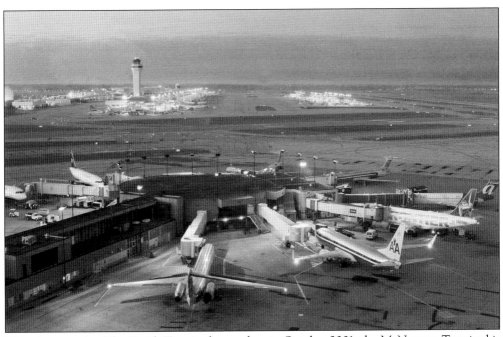

This photograph of the Smith Terminal was taken in October 2001; the McNamara Terminal is in the foreground. The Smith terminal was retired in 2008 with the opening of the new North Terminal. (VP.)

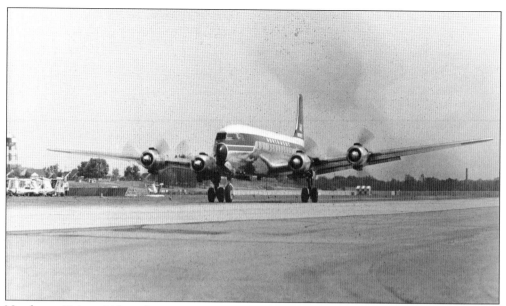

Northwest Orient Airlines began operations at Detroit Metro in 1958. By the 1980s, Northwest had expanded to Europe and used Detroit Metro as a major hub. It dropped Orient from its name soon after purchasing Republic Airlines in 1986. (NWA.)

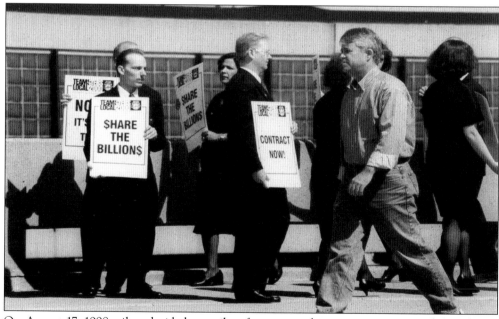

On August 17, 1998, pilots decided to strike after not reaching an agreement with Northwest Airlines. They believed that after helping Northwest out of bankruptcy in 1993 they deserved more money in this instance. Pres. Bill Clinton was not going to get involved, but after public demand he ordered the pilots back to both work and the negotiating tables on September 1, 1998. (WCAA.)

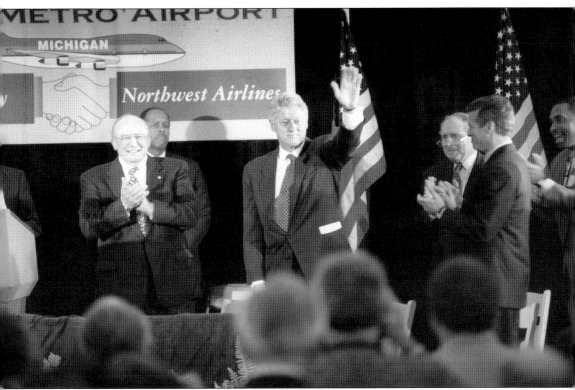

On October 21, 1996, Pres. Bill Clinton was on hand with Wayne County Executive Edward McNamara (second from the left) for the ground-breaking of the new 74-gate Midfield Terminal. According to the 1998 Project Development Agreement (PDA) between Northwest Airlines and Detroit Metro Airport, the original Midfield project cost estimate was $710,789,000. In 1998, before the initial bonds were sold for the project, the first amendment to the PDA was signed, and the project cost rose to $1,080,057,000. Ground was then broken for the terminal. In 2002, another amended and restated PDA, which added on Phase II of the project, brought the total cost to $1,285,007,000. The new terminal opened in 2005 and was named the Edward McNamara Terminal. (WCAA.)

U.S. Department of Transportation
Federal Aviation Administration

AIRPORT OPERATING CERTIFICATE

This certifies that the WAYNE COUNTY AIRPORT AUTHORITY, *as operator of the* DETROI *METROPOLITAN WAYNE COUNTY AIRPORT, Detroit, Michigan, has met the requirements of t Federal Aviation Act of 1958, as amended, and the rules, regulations, and standards prescribed thereunder f the issuance of this certificate, and is hereby authorized to operate as a certificated airport in accordance w and subject to said Act and the rules, regulations, and standards prescribed thereunder, including but not limit to 14 CFR Part 139, and any additional terms, conditions, and limitations contained herein, or in the curren approved Airport Certification Manual on file with the Federal Aviation Administration. This Certificate is n transferable and, unless sooner surrendered, suspended or revoked, shall continue in effect.*

Effective Date: **May 21, 1973**   *By Direction of the Administrator*
Issued at: **Des Plaines, Illinois**
               August 9, 2002

Manager, Airports Division

In an effort to improve efficiency of the operation of Detroit Metro Airport and Willow Run Airport, the Michigan State Legislature created the Wayne County Airport Authority (signed into law on March 26, 2002, Public Act 90) as an independent agency to oversee both airports; operational authority was transferred from Wayne County to the Wayne County Airport Authority that year. The airports were always self-funded and not supported by taxes. The airport authority is overseen by a board appointed jointly by the Wayne County executive, the Wayne County Commission, and the Michigan government. (WCAA.)

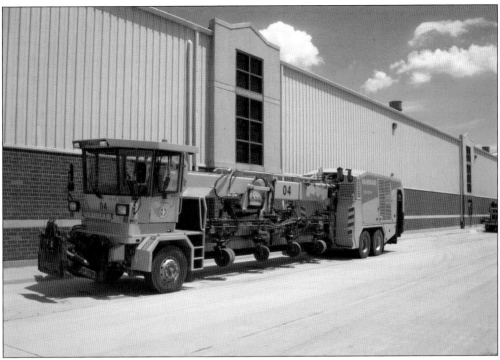

The snow-removal machine above, built by Vammas, has a snowplow in front, a street-sweeper mechanism in the center, and a blower in the back. No salt is used on the runways during the winter, which is incompatible with aircraft and can get sucked into jet engines—obviously, that could create many problems. With a fleet of snow-removal equipment, the maintenance personnel keep the airport running smoothly. (Above, author's collection; below, WCAA.)

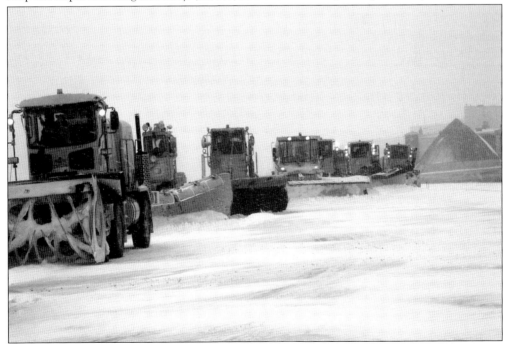

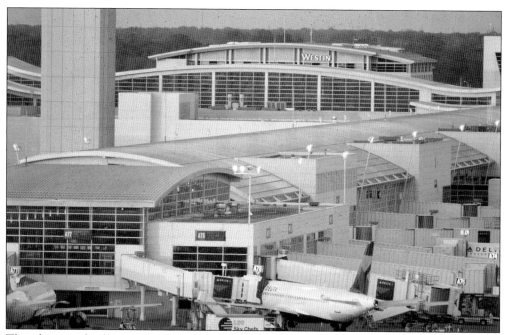

This photograph offers a view of the McNamara Terminal looking southeast. It is home to Delta Air Lines' second largest hub and is its gateway to the Pacific. The Westin hotel, visible in the background, has 414 rooms and is the only hotel at the airport attached to the terminal. (VP.)

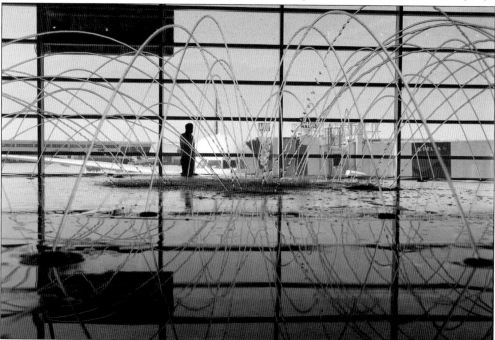

This fountain was designed specifically for the McNamara Terminal by WET Design, a California-based company. It has already been used in a few movies and commercials filmed at the airport. The Michigan Film Incentive Program has brought many filmmakers to Detroit Metro; the two vacant terminals make the airport ideal for filming without interruption from spectators. (VP.)

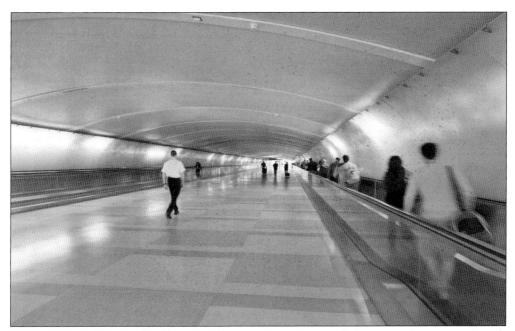

There is an underground walkway at the McNamara Terminal that joins Concourse A with Concourses B and C. Fox Fire Glass of Pontiac, Michigan, created the glasswork, and Mills James Productions of Columbus, Ohio, developed the illumination and music. (VP.)

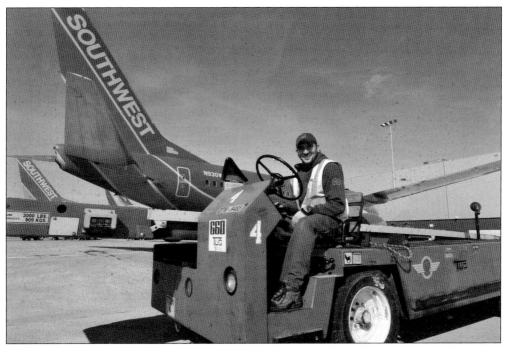

As of 2010, there were more than 18,000 men and women working at Detroit Metro Airport. Of the 18,000, six hundred people are employed directly by the airport authority, and the rest work with the airlines, ground handlers (baggage, caterers, and fuelers), security, federal agencies, and other companies. (VP.)

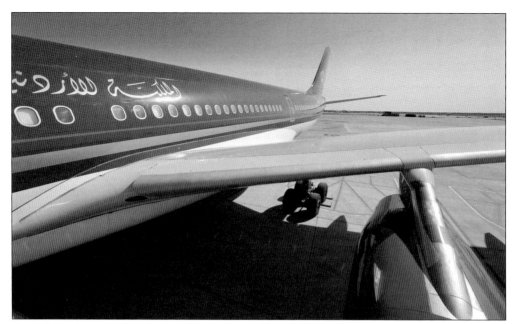

As of 2011, there are four foreign-flag carriers at Detroit Metro. Royal Jordanian Airlines is one of them; the airline only flies out of two other airports in the United States: New York (JFK) and Chicago (ORD). The flight at Metro connects Detroit with Amman, Jordan. (VP.)

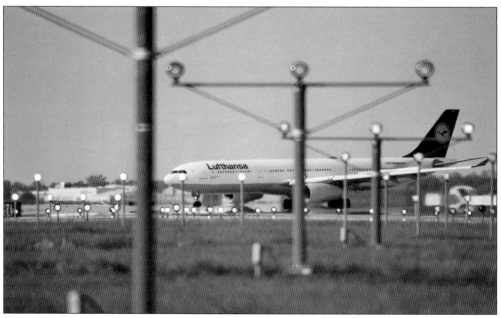

The other three foreign airlines are Lufthansa, Air France, and Air Canada. Lufthansa has daily trips to the airline's hub in Frankfurt, Germany. (VP.)

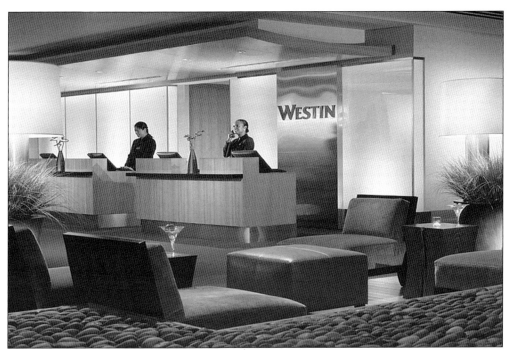

Since the airport opened, the facilities have offered rooms for weary travelers. Although there are about 10 hotels around the airport, the Westin is the only one connected to a terminal. In a test program, the Transportation Security Administration has allowed hotel guests who have been screened and allowed in the passenger terminal to walk around and enjoy the shops and restaurants. This is only allowed in a few other airports, and if it continues to work out it could be implemented nationwide. Below is a photograph of the Westin lobby. (VP.)

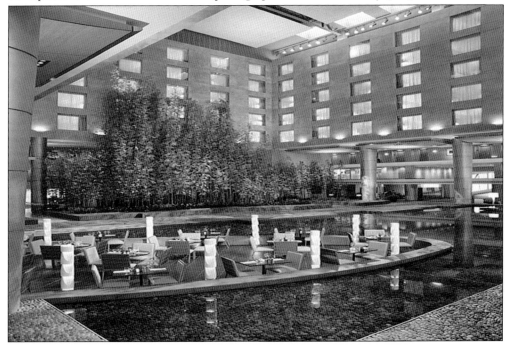

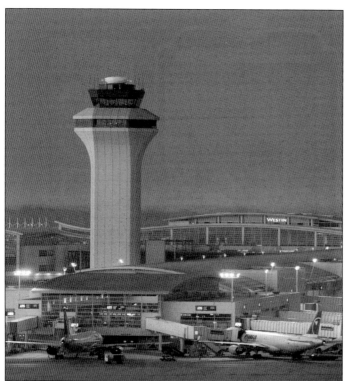

The control tower stands over 250 feet above the McNamara Terminal and is still the focal point of the airport. The view from the tower is spectacular—one can see the Renaissance Center in Detroit and the private planes taking off from Grosse Ile or Willow Run Airports. Viewers can even see the Fermi II nuclear power plant near Lake Erie. The controllers are top notch and can identify any aircraft that lands at Detroit Metro. (VP.)

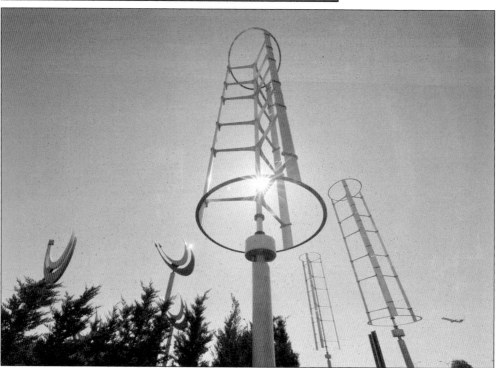

These wind turbines, manufactured in Michigan for Windspire Energy, were installed at the airport's north and south entrances on April 22, 2010 (Earth Day), as part of a test program. (VP.)

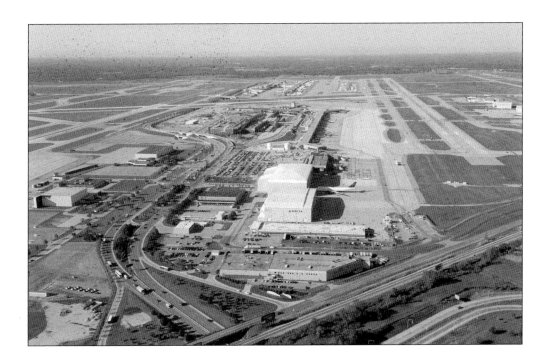

Above, a southward view of the airport displays the two large hangars occupied by Delta Air Lines and the old international terminal behind them. The road goes through the airport now, even though there is still a loop-around at the old Smith Terminal. Below is a northward view that shows the McNamara Terminal and the multistory parking structure. (VP.)

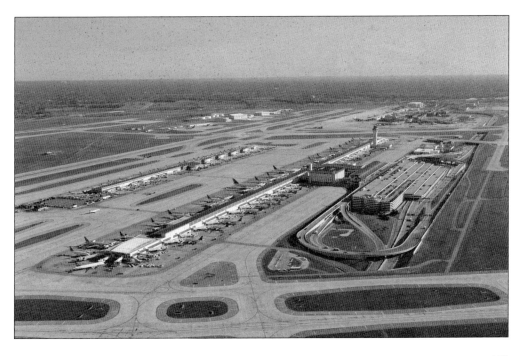

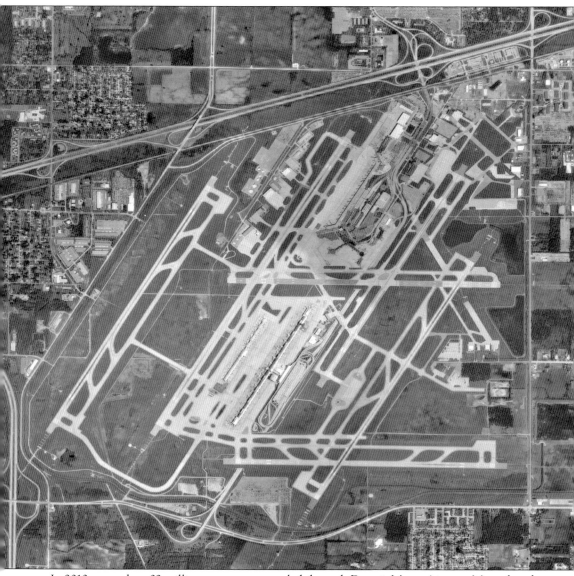

In 2010, more than 32 million passengers traveled through Detroit Metro Airport. Many decades later, the original portions of the airport are still utilized. The airport will continue to grow and modernize with the latest technologies, moving ahead to a bright future. (VP.)

BIBLIOGRAPHY

"Hijacking: Minute by Minute." The *Detroit Free Press*, November 12, 1972: A11.

"Hijackers Quizzed in Havana: FBI's gunplay assailed." The *Detroit News*, November 13, 1972: A1 and A10.

Pipp, Edwin G. "Burned In Jet Crash, Children Visit Base." *Detroit News*. December 21, 1959: A3.

Rickman, Sarah Byrn. *The Originals: The Women's Auxiliary Ferrying Squadron of World War II.* Saratoga, FL: Disc-Us Books, Inc., 2001.

Scharr, Adela Riek. *Sisters in the Sky: Volume I: The WAFS.* St. Louis: The Patrice Press, 1986.

Wayne County Road Commission Annual Road Reports: 1928, 1929, 1930, 1931, 1932, 1938, 1939, 1941, 1947, 1949, 1950, 1951, 1952, 1954, 1955, 1958, 1959, 1961, 1966.

DISCOVER THOUSANDS OF LOCAL HISTORY BOOKS
FEATURING MILLIONS OF VINTAGE IMAGES

Arcadia Publishing, the leading local history publisher in the United States, is committed to making history accessible and meaningful through publishing books that celebrate and preserve the heritage of America's people and places.

Find more books like this at
www.arcadiapublishing.com

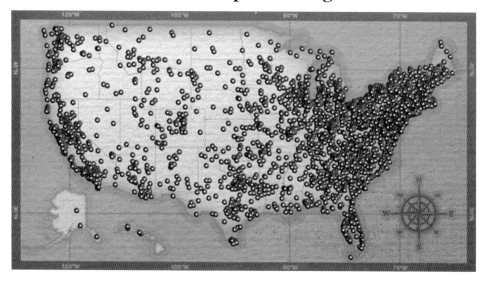

Search for your hometown history, your old stomping grounds, and even your favorite sports team.

Consistent with our mission to preserve history on a local level, this book was printed in South Carolina on American-made paper and manufactured entirely in the United States. Products carrying the accredited Forest Stewardship Council (FSC) label are printed on 100 percent FSC-certified paper.

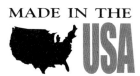
MADE IN THE USA